In *Thrive*, Meenoo Rami does an amazing job of turning the challenges of teaching in this new, networked world of learning into opportunities for teachers and students alike. She shares an amazing array of practical ideas that will help both veteran and brand-new teachers find support and inspiration for working in the technology-rich environments that the modern learner demands. Filled with stories of real teachers in real classrooms to support her ideas, Meenoo's book is simply a must-read for any educator wanting to better understand the potentials for student and personal learning in this most complex and exciting time.

> —*Will Richardson, author of* Why School? How Education Must
> Change When Learning and Information Are Everywhere

Whether you are entering your first year teaching or your fortieth, *Thrive* feels as if it were written just for you. At a time in our profession when many of us are feeling stretched thin, Meenoo Rami offers wisdom and practical strategies to reignite our passions and rediscover why we chose to teach. From rethinking mentor–mentee structures to building networks of inspiration to empowering yourself and your students to design your own instruction, this book is an invitation to innovate in your personal practice and in our profession.

> —*Christopher Lehman, author of* Falling in Love with Close Reading

Thrive is a primer for reflective practice. Meenoo Rami offers us a path for individualized professional development, teacher empowerment, and career longevity. Meenoo's voice rings with authority and passion from every page— inspiring! A rich resource for novices and veterans alike, *Thrive* is a must-own title for every professional educator.

> —*Donalyn Miller, author of* The Book Whisperer *and* Reading in the Wild

Regardless of one's profession, it is important to cultivate a practice of evaluating and re-evaluating progress and personal growth. Meenoo Rami adeptly shares critical ways for educators to check in with themselves and track their progress, and to inject passion into their work. Her ideas are relevant for both rookie teachers and classroom veterans alike!

> —*Angela Maiers, consultant and Huffington Post blogger*

Teaching is a profession that eats its young. Meenoo Rami's *Thrive* offers guidelines for surviving the challenges of the classroom as well as the faculty room. This book is certain to save new teachers buckets of tears.

> —*Carol Jago, author, English teacher, and past president*
> *of the National Council of Teachers of English*

Meenoo Rami lives joy. She sees teachers and students as co-creators of vibrant, real, and exacting work. *Thrive* includes a mosaic of dynamic teacher voices from many grade levels and content areas. Reading their stories deepened my thinking about the immense untapped potential of our profession. *Thrive* is for new teachers seeking a wise mentor. It is for any teacher who imagines a bold approach to the challenge of reaching all children today. Meenoo Rami's vision of teaching and learning can sustain us all.

—Penny Kittle, author of Book Love

To be successful, teachers must constantly be learning, reflecting, and growing to meet the ever-changing needs of the students in front of them. To many of us, this can seem like an overwhelming task. Who do I learn from? How can I keep growing as an educator? How do I keep the work I do relevant and fresh to myself and my students? Fortunately, Meenoo Rami has written this book that provides a road map for all of us to, yes, thrive, in our schools over the course of a career. And as Meenoo's principal, I can say that she lives the words of this book in her classroom every day.

—Chris Lehmann, Founding Principal, Science Leadership Academy

Meenoo Rami has written the right book at the right time. In an era of corporate education reform, *Thrive* reminds us of how we, as teachers, need human interaction, intellectual fulfillment, and empathy just as much as our students. Rami encourages us to move beyond the mechanical acts of scripted schooling and mandatory professional development, offering us numerous ways to pursue our own passions and bring them to the classroom. She notes that "the rewards of this work will be paid with your students' success and engagement." Filled with practical suggestions, stories from fellow educators, and smart questions, *Thrive* will reward you as a reader, too.

—Troy Hicks, author of Crafting Digital Writing

Meenoo Rami has written the book I would want to give to all new teachers, young and old, to show them teaching can blossom into a fulfilling profession, rich in human connection and intellectual passion. And her five strategies that help teachers to thrive will resonate with engaged teachers everywhere and are as true for the seasoned veteran as the newcomer.

—Elyse Eidman-Aadahl, National Writing Project Director

This is the book I wish I had been able to read when I began teaching. On every page Meenoo offers practical suggestions, accompanied by wit and wisdom, that can help us solve the problems we all encounter no matter how long we have been teaching. Thanks to her vision and her voice, I see great hope in the future for our profession.

—from the Foreword by Jim Burke

MEENOO RAMI

THRIVE

5 Ways to (Re)Invigorate Your
TEACHING

Foreword by **Jim Burke**

HEINEMANN
Portsmouth, NH

Heinemann
361 Hanover Street
Portsmouth, NH 03801–3912
www.heinemann.com

Offices and agents throughout the world

The author and publisher wish to thank those who have generously given permission to reprint borrowed material:

Figure 2–1: Photo by Karen Blumberg

Library of Congress Cataloging-in-Publication Data
Rami, Meenoo.
   Thrive : 5 ways to (re)invigorate your teaching / Meenoo Rami ; foreword by Jim Burke.
       p. cm.
   Includes bibliographical references.
   ISBN: 978-0-325-04919-9
   1. Middle school teaching—Handbooks, manuals, etc. 2. High school teaching—Handbooks, manuals, etc. I. Title.

LB1735.5.R36 2014
371.102—dc23   2013040949

Editor: Tobey Antao
Production: Victoria Merecki
Typesetter: Eric Rosenbloom, Kirby Mountain Composition
Cover and interior designs: Monica Ann Crigler
Manufacturing: Steve Bernier

Printed in the United States of America on acid-free paper
18 17 16 15 14 VP 2 3 4 5

In loving memory of my dad, Dr. Kanti Rami

For teaching me about the power of words and
inspiring me to make a difference with them

To my sister, Juie Rami

For always being there for me

Let the beauty we love be what we do.
There are hundreds of ways to kneel and kiss the ground.

—Jalaluddin Rumi

Contents

Foreword

In this new era of teaching, we all face challenges and demands that, more than ever, we cannot hope to meet on our own. They are too many, too complex. We need to build networks and share our knowledge with other professionals throughout the country who face the same obstacles and opportunities; we need to create, contribute to, and learn from many such communities and conversations. In this book, Meenoo Rami shares her experiences participating in an array of professional organizations and communities, online and off, and provides details about how we can join in.

Meenoo offers us all, new and experienced teachers alike, a compelling and thoughtful guide to our work as teachers. The 140 (typographical) characters Twitter limits her to as the founder and moderator of #engchat become, in *Thrive*, the 140 (human) characters she has read, learned from, been mentored by, and taught during her first years as a teacher at an urban interdisciplinary public high school in Philadelphia. What strikes me most is the degree to which her discussion of the people who have shaped her overlooks the degree to which she herself has become, in a very short time, a mentor to teachers across the country through her example as a teacher and leader.

In Chapter 1, Meenoo discusses all the ways in which we can be mentored and the processes by which we might find the mentors we need at various stages in our career. She offers interesting and insightful profiles of various types of mentors: "the mentor who helps me fine-tune my instruction," "the mentor who dares me into new work," and "the mentor who helps me see what's possible in my writing life," for example. She pays me the honor of singling me out in the latter role, but in doing so she highlights something she discusses elsewhere in the chapter: we must each seek out our own mentors, asking them how to do certain things, how to think about other things, how they were able to achieve something we have now decided we, too, wish to do but cannot do without their guidance. What Meenoo is far too humble to recognize or say out loud is that through the public forums she has created for herself, she has become the mentor who shows us all what it looks like to be what author Susan Cain calls a "quiet leader" and others call a "thought leader," as well as the mentor who shows older teachers how to work with and learn from the new generation of teachers.

A deep, rich portrait of our profession emerges in the pages of this book, a portrait that embodies the best of what David Whyte refers to as "the three marriages"—to our work; to the larger tradition of which our work is a part; and to our personal, sacred lives. Meenoo offers insights throughout about how to make these "marriages" work, make them last, make them *thrive*.

This is the book I wish I had been able to write years ago when I sent a hodgepodge manuscript to Heinemann with the catchy title *The First Five Years*, my premise being that I had, despite all the usual challenges, thrived in my work and had useful ideas to offer. Only when one has written a book, however, does one realize what is involved in writing a book worth publishing, worth the time it takes to read. At that point, I knew how to write but not what to say. Meenoo knows how to write and has something important to say; I wish I had been able to read this book when I began teaching so long ago (guided by my remarkable mentors Pat Hanlon, Rosemary Patton, and Bill Robinson). On nearly every page Meenoo generously and humbly does what she does every day online and in her school: offers practical suggestions, accompanied by wit and wisdom, that can help us solve the problems we encounter no matter how long we have been teaching. Throughout this gem of a book, Meenoo invites us to learn, to listen, and to lead—as she no doubt does every day to the 140-plus (student) characters who enter her classroom. Both within and outside her classroom, Meenoo Rami wants us all, her colleagues and students, not just to survive but to *thrive*. Thanks to this book and her example, that elusive ideal is now more attainable. For that hope, and for Meenoo, I am so very grateful: thanks to her vision and her voice, I see great hope in the future for our profession.

Jim Burke
Author of *The English Teacher's Companion*

Acknowledgments

I am deeply indebted to all those who I have come in contact with while on my journey as a learner and as a teacher. Many thanks to countless teachers, who I have met through workshops, presentations, conferences, Twitter chats, and email exchanges—they have pushed my thinking around the ideas presented in this book. It would be impossible to name all of them here but their influence on me is indisputable.

To my teachers, Dr. Venegoni at John Hersey High School and Dr. Greene at Bradley University—thank you for helping me fall in love with learning. You helped me get started on this journey a long time ago.

I'd like to express my thanks to my students and colleagues at the Science Leadership Academy, especially the class of 2013 and the class of 2014, for letting me learn with you and learn from you while writing this book. Thank you to my colleagues who have generously shared their craft and insights, and gave encouragement when I needed it most. Special thanks to Chris Lehmann, for creating the type of community at SLA where a teacher's voice is valued and contribution to our profession is celebrated.

I found my voice through the encouragement of the National Writing Project community, especially Elyse Eidman-Aadahl, Paul Oh, and Christina Cantrill. I'd also like to acknowledge the Philadelphia Writing Project for inspiring me to share my ideas with a wider audience. Also, thank you to other organizations such as the National Council of Teachers of English and the Center for Teaching Quality for giving me a public space to share my ideas.

I'd like to thank every member of the #engchat community for being part of this awesome community of English teachers on the web. I look forward to continuing to learn from you and with you.

A special thanks to all of these teachers who share their stories in the forthcoming pages. Without your input, this work would be incomplete:

- Kira Baker Doyle
- Joshua Block
- Christopher Bronke
- Russ Goerend
- Sarah Gross
- Terry Erickson

- Mary Beth Hertz
- Jennifer Isgitt
- Katie McKay
- Gamal Sherif
- Rita Sorrentino
- John T. Spencer
- Meredith Stewart
- Jose Vilson
- Luke Zeller

Thank you to Tobey Antao for seeing the possibility of this book before I did. From our very first breakfast meeting to the very last stages of production of this book, you have been a thoughtful guide in this process. Thank you for supporting and encouraging me through the lowest and highest points of the writing process. Your keen insights and questions have helped shape the direction and vision of this book.

I'd like to thank Heinemann publishing, especially Vicky Boyd, Lisa Fowler, Monica Crigler, Suzanne Heiser, Patty Adams, Anthony Marvullo, Shannon Thorner, Sarah Fournier, Victoria Merecki, Kim Cahill, and Kerry Herlihy.

Finally, I'd like to thank my sister Juie Rami, for being a steady force of strength, courage, inspiration, support, and encouragement in my life.

Introduction

During my first few years as a teacher, a couple of times a year, a string of bad days would haunt me at school. During these days, it was difficult to fight the feelings of isolation, the sense that I was having no positive impact on my students; there were even curt interactions with students where I was left feeling that my work was not being appreciated by students, their parents, or the school community. The worst feeling was the sense that my students and I were just going through the motions of playing school rather than actually creating meaningful work together. The sheer exhaustion from long days of teaching, grading, and planning would leave me depleted, and I would have to push myself to find the strength to continue giving my best effort to my students. However, sometimes my best effort would not even be enough, and I would have this dreadful feeling that I wasn't fully prepared to teach on that particular day. Giving anything less than best learning experiences to my students would leave me ridden with guilt. These feelings would often last more than a day; they would take over my mind and spirit for a while. I would question my decision to enter the classroom and generally feel like I had gotten lost at some point in my life and maybe had taken a wrong turn to arrive here in a classroom. I didn't know then that these feelings were common among first year teachers and the reason why so many leave the profession early in their careers.

Slowly, I discovered my own power to find meaning, solve complex problems, and make meaningful connections that inspire me to this very day. This slow evolution as an empowered teacher happened because of a few very specific experiences: I joined communities like the National Writing Project and National Council for Teachers of English. I met mentors like Jim Burke and Chris Lehmann, and I started contributing to my field by starting conversations about teaching and learning through Twitter. These experiences helped me feel less alone and armed me with a variety of new tools and ideas that helped my students and let me see my practice with new eyes. This transformation did not happen overnight, and in the forthcoming chapters, I share some of what I learned with you.

I am not the luckiest teacher in the world, and the success I have experienced in my brief career is not accidental. What I have done is ask for help relentlessly; I have begged, borrowed, and stolen great ideas from teachers in my professional network. Fearlessly, I have tried new ideas and have asked my students to go on a journey of learning that is often a meandering path rife with uncertainties and discomfort. I have trusted my students to take on challenging and meaningful work that resonates with their personal interests, investments, and inquiries.

In this book I present a paradigm of teacher leadership and ways in which teachers are addressing their own professional development needs. However, the suggestions presented in this book should not be seen as a panacea. The specific context in which you work will determine the type of approach you will take to address your own need for meaning. I have reached out to many teachers to contribute their experiences to this book because the principles outlined in this book are bigger than just my personal experience. As a result, you will find voices from teachers in schools from urban, suburban, and rural parts of our country spanning the K–12 spectrum. Some of these teachers are veterans, while others have only a few years of experience in the classroom. Each voice offers a unique inside look at the journey toward becoming an empowered teacher. Each chapter in this book offers snippets from these classrooms and the work teachers are doing to address their own needs as professionals.

- **Chapter 1: Turn to Mentors**
  This chapter pays homage to the important role mentors play in our lives. It focuses on finding mentors and ways that you can maintain these relationships in your life.

- **Chapter 2: Join and Build Networks**
  This chapter is a nod to the power of networks and how teachers can locate relevant networks, seek support within them, and also contribute to them in meaningful ways.

- **Chapter 3: Keep Your Work Intellectually Challenging**
  This chapter defies the notion that those who cannot do, teach. Teaching is an intricate web of interconnected factors, and at its center, you as the teacher make important decisions that impact your students' learning experience.

- **Chapter 4: Listen to Yourself**
  This chapter is an attempt to help you remember who you are and provides ways you can align your values about teaching and learning with the decisions you make in your classroom.

- **Chapter 5: Empower Your Students**
  This chapter brings all other ideas presented in this book and helps you find ways you can empower your students. The ultimate task for you as a teacher is to leave your students more curious and courageous. This chapter is all about doing just that.

In this book, I have tried to describe my stance on teaching and learning and how it has helped me thrive in the classroom. At once personal and applicable to teachers at all experience levels, these chapters capture snapshots from the classroom and provide concrete ways that will help you connect with a larger community of practitioners who grapple with the complexity of our work. As author and teacher Kelly Gallagher says, you can teach for twenty years or you can teach the same year twenty times. This is a book for those who want to see their practice through new eyes, and want to proudly share their teaching craft with others. By doing the very same things this book proposes, I have found hope, strength, and courage to come back to teaching year after year. This book is written for those who are looking to continue to grow their practice no matter how long they have been teaching. Lastly, it asks you to take a leadership role in our profession by mentoring and supporting others and by making your work public. It is an effort to restore respect for our profession and recognize the complexity in the craft of teaching.

On a rare occasion, I still face one of those days I experienced frequently in my first year of teaching, but for the most part, I find joy in the work I do everyday alongside my students. Most days, I look forward to heading to school and continuing the work I've started with my students. Being around students, colleagues, parents, and visitors to my school energizes me, and encourages me to keep going no matter how difficult the task seems at times.

Through my work, I have found a way to bring all of myself into the classroom and align seemingly disparate parts of myself in my role as a teacher, mentor, and guide. I have finally understood the words of Persian poet Rumi: "When you do things from your soul, you feel a river moving in you, a joy." In other words, I have gone from wanting to merely survive the struggles of the classroom to thriving as an educator. While I might still struggle at times with motivation, finding meaning, and locating resources, I have amassed the tools I need to keep building the path of my own progress. I hope these tools help you thrive in your own classroom and empower the students you teach each day.

CHAPTER 1

Turn to Mentors

If I have seen further it is by standing on the shoulders of giants.

—Isaac Newton, letter to Robert Hooke

When I started teaching, I was twenty-six years old. Not as green as I would have been at twenty-two, but still I had unsure footing as I took my first steps into my first classroom: room 204. Upon entering the room, I noticed the beautiful, polished hardwood floor, the water-damaged blackboard, and desks piled on top of each other in the corner. Moments before, after teaching a sample lesson, my principal Mr. Gotlieb had offered me the position on the spot. For the previous two years, I had worked full time at City Year while going to graduate school at Temple University. After seeing Philadelphia schools up close through my work at City Year, I was inspired to teach and not just complain about the state of urban education over beers with my friends. As I looked around my new classroom that first day, I knew that first year of teaching would be difficult, but I had no idea of the challenges I would face.

I was not prepared to teach 165 students in classes ranging from English 1–4. I quickly realized that I would need a great deal of support in the upcoming months as I became acclimated to the work set before me. At the end of the teaching day, I would try to piece together what had actually happened—how had things gone that day? What did I need to prepare for the next day to make it a better one? I would be at school as late as 8 or 9, trying to remember what class had been assigned what reading and who needed to make up vocab quizzes that week; the sheer management of all the individual adjustments my students needed on assignments was beyond my control at that point in the day. I would go home, my bag stuffed with my laptop, papers, and novels, to continue grading or revising lesson plans. I didn't know what the phrase dog-tired meant till that year.

Amongst these challenges, one of the supports offered by my district was a new teacher coach. Every new teacher in the district was assigned a coach to help us make a smooth transition into our first year as teachers. My mentor, a member of the New Teacher Coach Cohort, visited me a number of times during that year. She would usually come on Thursday mornings and I remember that I was using the text *The House on Mango Street* with ninth-grade students and we were working toward writing our own collection of vignettes about people from our own neighborhoods. We used Cisneros' work as a mentor text to learn how to tell a story with sensory details. While I was assured that she was not there to judge me or report me to the administration, I was filled with fear of having her in the classroom. I was falling short of my own expectations as a teacher, and I felt shame about having a stranger watch me fail, at least in my eyes. As time went on, I did my best to be open to feedback I was receiving from my coach, such as improving my wait time during discussion, and the general encouragement that my performance was perfectly fine for a new teacher. My coach was trying to help, but the feedback that she offered was not what I needed at the time, and I didn't know how to ask her for the help I desperately needed.

I was not alone in this situation.

When you compare this mentorship I received as a first-year teacher—typical in structure and expectations for many new teachers—to the years that master craftsmen once spent training apprentices in a trade, you can see why many new teachers feel that they are going it alone or that working with a mentor is just one more hurdle as they strive for independence. While the idea of mentoring goes all the way back to apprenticeships in the Middle Ages, today's assigned mentorships are often a far cry from those relationships. Currently, most programs that prepare teachers for the classroom require only 12–16 weeks of student teaching under the supervision of a cooperative teacher, and mentorship or coaching programs for first-year teachers can vary greatly in terms of intensity.

But the research suggests that teachers who have had a more varied mentorship experience are more likely to thrive in their work and to stay in the field. According to fifteen empirical studies about mentoring reviewed by University of Pennsylvania professor and researcher Richard Ingersoll, teachers who received mentoring support "performed better at various aspects of teaching, such as keeping students on task, developing workable lesson plans, using effective student questioning practices, adjusting classroom activities to meet students' interests, maintaining a positive classroom atmosphere, and demonstrating successful classroom management" (2012, 51). He also concluded that student teachers who participated in "some kind of induction" had "higher scores, or gains, on academic achievement tests" (51). The study concluded that teachers who fared best of all had a "comprehensive package" (51) of mentoring, which included meetings with peers and planning with other teachers in their subject area. However, only about five percent of new teachers are getting support for that kind of mentorship from their administration. As a result, thousands of teachers leave the profession because they feel a lack of support in their school communities. There is strong evidence that as many as fifty-six percent left the profession, "citing job dissatisfaction and a desire to find an entirely new career" (Kopkowski 2008). But, strong mentoring has shown to reduce beginning teacher attrition activities such as "on-the-job observations and coaching in the classroom as well as support for teacher planning by expert veterans" (Darling-Hammond).

This is a sad reality, but some teachers like Terry Erickson, a fourth-grade teacher in Edina, MN, get lucky and find a mentor early on in their path. He remembers Diana, the mentor that his district assigned him when he began teaching:

> She is an amazing teacher that I learned so much from during that first year. She always made time for me no matter how busy her life was at the time. She would show not tell. She would tell me stories about her own teaching experiences and what she learned from them instead of giving me suggestions or ideas that I could do. In other words, I learned from her experience. . . . We still see each other and talk when we have time. In fact I am meeting with her next week to plan a collaborative read aloud project with our students via Skype.

Unlike Terry, after my first year of mentorship, I felt less than empowered. Spending time with my mentor had not prepared me to solve my own problems or know where to turn for guidance or direction once her assigned time in my class was over. I believe many teachers have this reaction. If they've had mentorships that felt more bureaucratic than personalized, it might feel liberating to be on their own. If they've had mentors who have functioned more like supervisors, they might feel that they have earned their stripes. However, in spite of the range of emotions, this one-size-fits-all model may leave many new teachers isolated with their work. In this crucial time when learning is still happening so quickly, we start to understand what we need. We may have some aspects of our jobs that we'd like to get better at but don't quite know how to, or we might worry the work is starting to feel stale. I realized that I didn't want to be mentor-free. Instead, I needed mentors who were going to energize me. I also realized I was going to have to find them myself.

Julie Jee @mrsjjee

It's so helpful if the coach/mentor's heart is in the right place. Plenty of people are assigned mentees = often disastrous. #ntchat

5:04 pm—3/28/2012

Joan Young @Flourishingkids

@mrsjjee So true, my former intern who works at a different school than I, has an assigned mentor now who is not a great match :-(#ntchat

5:06 PM—3/28/2012

What Mentoring *Could* Be

Today, my relationships with my mentors look very different from the version of mentorship I first received as a new teacher. I don't have just one mentor; I have over half a dozen. My mentors aren't all part of my school community. One of my mentors is two time zones away, and one isn't even in the field of education. My mentors are not perfectly compatible with every aspect of my job: Two teach English in schools that are very different from mine and one teaches a different subject and a different grade level. My mentors don't just give me answers: some help me respond to pressing needs from a position of experience or work with me as I try out new ideas. These mentors don't fit the mold of mandated mentorship, but, I have found that each of these people have been invaluable models and guides for particular parts of my professional and personal life.

My mentors also have some things in common: all of them are people who I communicate with; they're not just people I admire from afar. All of them are people I respect. All of them are willing to field questions from me when I'm looking for answers. All of them are generous about sharing their experiences. All of them are people I trust enough to share my own concerns and worries with, as well as my successes. While some of the people on my list might consider me their mentee, others might consider me to be a colleague or a friend. The important part about having mentors isn't that we have formal roles, it's that my mentors are helping me in the ways that I want and need to grow.

The Mentor Who Helps Me See What's Possible in My Practice: **Chris Lehmann**

Chris is the founding principal of my school, Science Leadership Academy in Philadelphia, PA. It might seem strange to list my boss as a mentor, but Chris always finds time to have a dialogue about what I need, plans I'm making for my classes, or what doesn't sit well with me in my professional life. His door is always open—I can walk in, have a seat, and ask a question whenever I need to. Once, when I was struggling with how to respond to an irate email from a parent regarding a situation I had no power to resolve, I turned to Chris to help me formulate a response and avoided a miscommunication in the process. In these types of situations, he calms me down, validates my frustration while helping me find my own way out of challenging moments. Chris gives me direct, honest feedback, and he challenges me to think about what my students need and what I can be doing differently to help them.

The Mentor Who Helps Me Fine-Tune My Instruction: **Alexa Dunn**

A few years ago, it might also have been fair for me to call Alexa "The Mentor Who Helps Me Find the Paper for the Copier." When I started teaching at Science Leadership Academy, I had years of classroom experience, but I had no idea where to find the office supplies, how to submit my grades, or who to ask for help. Alexa, my fellow twelfth-grade English teacher and a founding faculty member at SLA, shared her vast institutional knowledge generously. She made sure that I had all of the support I needed, checking in with me often to see if I had any questions, large or small.

Alexa and I now visit each other's classrooms, giving each other feedback about what we're seeing. We share the joy and challenge of teaching twelfth graders, and we often adapt similar strategies in our classes to keep students motivated and engaged. Thanks to her keen insights, I've been making my classes more interactive, including having students share their ideas about writing topics using a speed-dating format. And, yes, I also know where the copy paper is now.

The Mentor Who Dares Me Into New Work: **Ann Leaness**

Ann, a high school English teacher in Philadelphia and one of the founders of Edcamp, is relentless in her drive to keep her work in the classroom interesting, both for herself and for her students. Ann and I might not see each other face-to-face very often, but in our emails, phone calls, and Google Docs collaborations, we have planned units and year-long overviews together. This past year, we came up with the idea of having our students experience authentic writing practices by publishing a collaborative teen magazine. Ann is selfless in sharing resources and ideas, and she expects the same from me. She's constantly asking, "What are you doing? What are your kids doing right now?" Working with Ann pushes me to see my practice through a new lens.

The Mentor Who Helps Me Find a Community: **Mary Beth Hertz**

What can a high school English teacher learn from an elementary technology coordinator? A lot. When I was teaching in a more traditional school, Mary Beth helped me to connect with Philadelphia educators who share my progressive vision of teaching and learning—people who weren't in my building, but were in my community. As a co-founder of Edcamp, Mary Beth understands the value of sharing ideas, even if we don't always know exactly where the sharing will lead. Conversations with Mary Beth have helped me to see how teachers can direct their own learning.

The Mentor Who Helps Me See What's Possible in My Writing Life: **Jim Burke**

I've known Jim's work for many years—the English Companion Ning and his books, especially What's the Big Idea? (2010), have been instrumental in my teaching practice. After I contacted Jim to ask him to host #engchat, I had a chance to get to know him personally, as well. Over the past few years, Jim has made time to talk with me about the future of teaching and about my own professional writing life. He is generous with his insights and gives me the long view in the field—something that I am still working on at this point in my career. I don't talk to Jim every week or even every month, but when we talk, he is truly present, and he helps me think hard about what it is that I want to do and how I can accomplish it.

The Mentor Who Helps Me Share My Work Publicly: **Christina Cantrill**

I first connected with Christina, a program associate at the National Writing Project, at a Philadelphia Writing Project summer institute. She was one of the first people to tell me that the work that I was doing in the classroom was interesting and worth sharing—a boost that has been incredibly important to me. She has invited me to present and write for the NWP many times, often suggesting ideas or setting up interesting collaborations. Her faith in me and in my work has helped me to value my own contribution to the profession.

The Mentor Who Helps Me Stay Balanced: **Juie Rami**

> I am lucky to have so many passionate, brilliant mentors in my field, but I am also grateful for my sister, Juie, who reminds me that I am not my job, my title, my accomplishments, or my failures. When I am facing a big decision or when I am anxious about a big presentation, Juie reminds me to have fun with the work that I am doing and helps me decide when to say yes and when to say no.

In the opening chapter of *Meditations*, Marcus Aurelius, a Roman Philosopher-King, lists things he has learned from family members, teachers, and friends. He is not only paying his respects but writing those things down to remember those lessons for later. As I write this, I am aware that I am a sum of all of my mentors. Whether personally or professionally, these men and women have helped me to be a better version of myself. Their collective impact cannot be separated from the cumulative effect on my growth as a person.

Finding Possible Mentors

You might already have an idea of who you'd like to mentor you, or you might be wondering where to begin. Either way, it can be helpful to push your thinking by considering the questions of potential mentors through a few different lenses:

What Do You Need?

"What do you need?" is a simple question, but it can elicit a lot of thinking. One way to begin is by identifying areas of interest:

- What am I curious about in my field?

- What are my students interested in that I would like to learn more about?

- What am I already doing well that I would like to get even better at?

Another starting point is identifying some sore spots. Take a deep breath and think about the following questions:

- What do I know, off the bat, that I would like to improve about my teaching practice?

- What have others (administrators, parents, even students) told me that I need to improve? Which of the suggestions seem to have merit?

- What drains my energy at work?

- Which of the goals that I had when I became a teacher am I still working on achieving?

- What would help me to feel more energetic about my work?

Finally, think about the kind of relationship you'd like to have with a mentor. You may want to decide upfront whether it is important to have a mentor who you are able to see face-to-face regularly or whether corresponding via email and using Skype is sufficient interaction for you. The right mentor for you may be teaching next door or may live across the country. You will need to decide how important proximity is for you in this relationship. Your relationship with your mentor may manifest in a monthly lunch, weekly coffee date, or merely an ongoing email exchange. Consider these questions:

- Do you need to talk in person, or would you be happy with online correspondence?

- Would it be enough to bounce ideas off of the person, or would you want the person to visit your class and provide feedback?

- How often would you want to be in touch with this person? Do you want someone to lend you an ear when you need to vent about the struggles you're facing?

- Do you want someone who will help with a specific issue or guide your career trajectory for the long-term?

Once you have an idea of the kind of support that you're looking for, you can start mining your most valuable natural resource: the people around you.

How Will You Find a Good Match?

You may find your mentor in your school, your professional network, or through a professional organization. If you consider who around you has a skill or focus that might be interesting to you, you might find mentors in unexpected places. For example, if you're a science teacher, you may not have much use for a neighboring history teacher's practice of using current headlines in class. However, you might want to know more about how she makes her content area meaningful to her students. You might even find that someone with whom you have disagreed in the past might be skilled in an area where you'd like to learn more. As you look at the questions below, try to assume a stance of genuine curiosity—where might you find help from both familiar faces and unfamiliar places?

In School

- Who seems to be passionate about their work and enjoy their job?

- Who lifts your spirits every time you see them in the halls?

- Who has students who excel?

- Who has students who trust them?

- Whose classes are full of engaged, energized students?

- Who is most likely to speak up in a staff meeting to say something that you agree with?

- Who is most willing to share ideas?

- Who has strong relationships with parents?

- Who has a quality that you would like to develop in yourself?

- Who has ideas that are fresh and interesting?

- Who is doing something that interests you but that you know nothing about?

- Whose career looks like a path you would like to follow?

Beyond Your Own School

- Who do you know who is able to do something you admire?

- Who is someone you have not yet met but who you could introduce yourself to—online or in person—who is doing something you admire?

Take a look at your list of wants and needs and the list of people you've brain-stormed. Who could help you learn about the things you want to learn about?

A few final questions:

- Is this a person I feel comfortable approaching for help?

- How does my personality and communication style compare to this person's personality and communication style? How could our personal style help my learning? How might they make mentoring challenging?

- Is this person someone I feel comfortable sharing my own concerns about my teaching with? For example, you might be concerned about asking your direct supervisor to be your mentor. This is not a set rule, of course: I con-sider my principal, Chris Lehmann, to be one of my mentors and he is my direct supervisor.

Mentors Could Be Anywhere

I'll admit, not every one of my mentorships was born of this careful calculation— for example, I met Christina Cantrill at one of my first experiences as a presenter, and she and I have been in touch ever since, sharing and developing ideas whenever one of us thinks the other will be interested. Christina has had an enormous ef-fect on my practice and my career. Sometimes, it's OK to just be lucky in finding a mentor.

However, we can't depend on fabulous mentors like Christina to appear out of nowhere. The kind of strategic thinking that I described above is what led me to muster up the courage to get in touch with Jim Burke. Jim had built an online community *and* he had managed to translate his practice into writing: two things that I was working on doing in my own life. When I introduced myself to him online with an invitation to host #engchat, I was nervous, but Jim was gracious, and I soon learned that he didn't mind fielding questions from me. His generosity with ideas and suggestions is amazing, and he's exactly the expert I want to turn to when I'm writing a book for teachers.

Reaching Out to a Potential Mentor

It can be intimidating to ask someone for help. However, it may be a great pleasure or honor for someone to know that you see her as such a person, and you will never know until you ask. It's always helpful to tell the person what you admire about his or her work or character and the reason why you specifically sought out this person's help. Finally, it's a good idea to be specific about the help you'd like. A few examples of how you might work with a mentor:

- Checking in with your mentor when you are facing a big decision or when you have a quick question.

- Finding time to see your mentor in action—sitting in on your mentor's class, or sitting beside your mentor to watch planning in action.

- Asking your mentor to talk through a specific issue with you.

- Inviting your mentor to observe you at work with a particular lens and to share his/her impressions and suggestions.

- Asking your mentor to recommend resources, books, and other tools.

A mentorship can be as formal or as casual as you and your mentor would like. Perhaps the word *mentor* might sound stiff to you—you might instead consider asking the person to grab coffee and talk through something with you or take a look at something you were planning on trying out with your class next week. Asking for advice on a specific situation and seeing how it sits with you might help to give you a feel for how a mentoring relationship might go. This one encounter may inform your decision about whether this person would be a good match for you as a mentor.

If things go well and it seems helpful to make the relationship more formal, you might want to plan out a schedule of times to talk or meet, or determine how the two of you should be in touch. If someone turns you down, don't take it personally: he may be too busy for this type of commitment and is being honest and up-front with you. Perhaps he can even recommend another potential mentor.

Remember, you don't need to rely on just one mentor. You can learn from a variety of people at once. As you get into the habit of asking people for this kind of help, you may find it more empowering and exciting than nerve-wracking.

Working with Mentors

The real challenge may come after you have secured a mentor. How do you maintain this relationship? Communicating clear expectations for time expected and area where you need support is paramount. Bringing your expertise and sharing what you know with your mentor makes the relationship more reciprocal and leaves both individuals feeling like they are benefiting from the time being invested.

Christopher's experience shows how mentorships can develop into collegial friendships that mutually benefit both people involved.

Profile

Christopher Bronke
English Department Chair
Downers Grove North High School, Illinois

I met my mentor as a freshman in high school as she was my English teacher. I guess you could make the case that the mentorship started at that point because she is the reason I have a love for English. The class for which she was my teacher was a regular-level English class, but at the end of the year she recommended that I should move into honors English. She was really the first person to see that in me, really seeing it in me before I even saw it in myself. Well, over the years we stayed in touch, including when I emailed her to let her know about my first job as an English teacher. I worked for seven years at two different high schools. I wanted a school that would push me to constantly be improving, so I reached out to her again. At this point, she had become department chair. She hired me, and I was then working for my mentor. Today, thanks to her guidance, she and I are now colleagues, each of us department chair at the two schools in the district.

I guess what is so powerful about the relationship is that we both trust one another and challenge one another. She doesn't treat me like a newbie, so to speak, but instead values my fresh take on things. I know that she is always there for me when I need advice, a second set of eyes, or just someone to listen while I bitch about my day. One of my fears in this situation is that I will let her down. Because of how much she has done for me, I hold her in such high regards, the last thing I want to do is disappoint her. That really is something that motivates me to constantly do my best.

When it is all said and done, I have gained a friend, a colleague, and a mentor.

Not every piece of advice will resonate with you and you don't have to adopt it and apply it to your life. You do not have to rely on one mentor alone. You can have a team of supporters and have different mentors for different areas of your professional life. Again, each of these relationships will be shaped by your specific needs and the time you invest in it. Finally, think about how you can show your gratitude for the time invested by your mentor in this relationship. Even a small token such as a hand-written thank-you note can leave an indelible impression of gratitude.

This relationship doesn't have to be one-sided; you're not merely there to just receive wisdom, advice, and guidance. You also bring valuable skills and qualities to the mentorship, share what you know. Perhaps you're very good at using online tools to automate the mundane tasks of life or you can perhaps share the way you use non-text-based prompts to promote writing in your class. No matter what your expertise is, no matter how small or big it may seem to you, be willing to share it with your mentor. You never know how you might become a source of inspiration and support for her as well.

I've Been Assigned a Mentor. Now What?

If I could go back in time and offer my new-teacher self some advice, I might remind myself that even if the assigned mentor didn't seem like a perfect fit for me, there are always things to study in a mentor. I might advise myself to learn what I could, and to take note of the things I did not want to emulate.

- Rather than relying on my mentor's general assurances that things were "fine," I could have asked for targeted feedback in areas that I knew I needed help in. For example, I might have asked my mentor: Would you watch the student with the striped shirt in the second row today? He's been alternately engaged and disengaged, and I'd like to try to pinpoint where he's getting lost.

- I've been working on how I'm closing my lessons. Would you pay special attention to that part of the period and let me know what you're thinking?

- I'm wondering if the way that I've been checking for understanding is as effective as it could be. Would you listen in on my questions and give me some suggestions at the end of the period?

- At the end of the period, would you give me a list of three things that you think I am doing well and three things that you think I could improve?

- I am wondering about _____. Would you suggest a resource to help me learn more about it?

Most importantly, remember that even if you have an assigned mentor, you can still look for the mentors you need.

———————————— ✖ ————————————

The great thing about our profession is that we have a tradition of mentorship at the core of it, whether you started teaching at twenty-two or at sixty-two, every student teacher is trained under the careful guidance of a cooperating teacher. This type of support doesn't have to end for you at the end of your fourteen-week stint in someone else's classroom. Your need for support will actually become apparent after you enter your own classroom and face your own challenges as an educator.

CHAPTER 2

Join and Build Networks

Educators must be more than information experts; they must be collaborators in learning, seeking new knowledge and constantly acquiring new skills alongside their students.

—U.S. Department of Education, *Transforming American Education: Learning Powered by Technology*

Under the right circumstances, groups are remarkably intelligent, and are often smarter than the smartest people in them.

—James Surowiecki, *The Wisdom of Crowds*

Our Google Docs are open and we're sitting together in the sunlit library on the second floor at the Science Leadership Academy. It's another Wednesday afternoon faculty meeting and this week we have finished writing narratives (reports that try to capture the achievements of our students in a longer form than a mere letter grade) and turning in third-quarter grades for our students. Our principal, Chris Lehmann, has asked us to use our meeting time to get together in small groups and look at our upcoming unit plans. He could use the time for a more typical, principal-led meeting, but his decision shows us all how much he values a community built on mutual trust and respect. He understands we all need a bit of energy to get us through the fourth quarter.

Melanie, a colleague in the Spanish department, looks at my unit plan on *The Crucible* and jots down comments: "These essential questions really push reflection." "This could lead to a really cool discussion about public and private space in-person and online." I get a chance to see how Melanie is incorporating art from Spain in her next teaching unit. I share with her the Google Art Project link, which allows students to virtually visit major museums in the world. This kind of collaboration is the foundation of my in-school network. They support my practice when I need new ideas; they question me and push me to see my students with new eyes. They challenge me by encouraging me to take even more risks toward student-led learning in my classroom. This network serves as my home base, my grounding for all the work I do as a teacher inside and outside of my classroom.

But I am not the only one who benefits from these ties. When a school has dense and interconnected relationships among its teachers, it increases its social capital as an organization. Look around any school that solves challenges collaboratively and successfully, you will find a group of teachers who are interconnected, interdependent, and committed to core values of the organization. It isn't surprising to learn that "Organizations with dense informal network structures within and between organizational units generally achieve higher levels of performance than those with sparse connections" (Reagans and Zuckerman 2001). Strong leaders within schools help the teachers see the value of true collaboration and help facilitate the process.

Not every school has a principal that fosters community as Chris does, but, like mentors, there are many networks that you can find on your own that will reenergize you on a daily basis with new ideas and help you fight the sense of isolation and fatigue that so many teachers feel. What we do every day is tremendously important and difficult but we also have the power to create a network of support as we continue to move ahead in this digital age which offers us so many possibilities.

The Importance of Connection

As the definition of an accomplished teacher evolves, we are grappling with what it means to teach and learn in today's world. However, one quality that seems essential is that an accomplished teacher must be connected. If we expect our students to be active, responsible, and independent digital and global citizens, we need to be models for them. If we are striving to create a system where the role of the teacher is no longer the lone expert in the room but a co-learner, we need to model that for our students, as well. As our access to technology increases, we have more ways to share ideas with our colleagues, collaborate on projects, learn from each other, and connect our students. This networking not only helps individual teachers, but schools as an organization as well. Kira Baker-Doyle, in her insightful book, *The Networked Teacher*, explains "the networks and communities that teachers build in schools are key mediating factors in determining the actual outcome of school reforms and in influencing teacher buy-in of new initiatives" (2011, 5).

This connection can be powerful when it extends beyond the physical limits of one school. The U.S. Department of Education published a report in 2011 called "Connect and Inspire: Online Communities of Practice in Education" in which researchers found that: "Online communities can support systematic, transformative change in teaching and learning." The report emphasized that connected, responsive, and welcoming online learning communities empower teachers in the following ways:

- **Access Knowledge**

  Teacher networks bring together expertise, tools, and thoughtful pedagogy. Networks build confidence for new teachers who are trying to gain a solid footing in their practice, and it gives experienced teachers a way to add new ideas and spirit to their practice. If we want our students to take advantage of free and quality resources for learning in our interconnected world, then we need to do the same and model lifelong learning for our students.

- **Create Knowledge**

  What might you create if you could work with collaborators who you choose because of your common interests or your expertise? When you join communities that are centered on a specific goal or interest, you put yourself into contact with people who are likely to energize you and your work. Suddenly, you and your team are in a position to create, not just consume, knowledge. What if you co-taught your current unit with someone across the hallway or across the country? What if your students interacted via blogs, chats, and created projects together? How would your instruction change if you became a learner in your class along with your students?

- **Share Knowledge**

  Joining a teacher network isn't just for the takers; it's for those who have something to give as well. Do your students love the way you break down multi-step variable equations problems? Know a fabulous way to introduce the Reconstruction Era in U.S. History? Can't sleep the night before you start your unit on *Romeo and Juliet* because you have a great plan for your students? Then you should be sharing your best ideas with your colleagues near and far so that they can learn from you and adapt what you are doing well for their students. Of course, we all grow individually year-by-year, but imagine the leaps we could make if we could leverage each other's work effectively.

◆ **Build Professional Identities, Relationships, and Collaboration**
Teacher networks provide a place for you to connect, build relationships, and reduce a sense of isolation as you navigate your career path. Along this path, role models, mentors, and colleagues will provide the guidance, support, and collegiality that keep us going even when our work is challenging.

Your Personal Network

A personal, or *ego-centric*, network is the ever-growing set of people you know. It includes your mentors, your colleagues, your students, their parents, your friends, your family, the people you chat with on Twitter, your doctor, and the friendly cashier at the grocery store who always has a comment about the weather. Some of the people in your network might not be the people you think of when you're trying to perfect your teaching practice. However, if we're working toward helping our students to see themselves as lifelong learners who can construct meaning from the world around them, your personal network might be a gold mine of experience and ideas.

While my students were studying the idea of the American Dream, I partnered up with the history teacher in my school and together we asked our students to apply the idea of the American Dream to their neighborhoods in Philadelphia, PA. We asked them to look at data points such as: poverty, education attained, access to public transportation, crime, and quality of schools. We wanted them to not only be able to understand the idea of the American Dream but also evaluate whether it is thriving in their neighborhoods. To help my students collect and understand this data, I was looking for someone with more expertise than myself in this area. When I mentioned this to my friend Nicole, she suggested that I connect with her friend, Michelle, who specializes in mapping data to make it more useful in finding trends, insights, and solutions. I would have never connected with Michelle if it were not for Nicole connecting us. My personal network has often helped me find a mentor for my students. I don't have to be the only person my students learn from; it is amazing to know how many people are willing to give their time and resources if you simply ask.

How Do You Get Started?

While it might be easy to bounce an idea off a friend, it might feel less simple to ask your cardiologist to come to class to discuss the workings of the circulatory system or to ask your accountant to visit and give context to recent economic developments. You might begin by framing your request with an acknowledgment of the person as an expert in his or her field. It's also helpful for people who have not taught to have a clear idea of what you have in mind in terms of time and involvement—would you like the person to address the class? To talk with a small group? To write an email that you'll share with your students? Consider these options as you begin to build your personal network.

Consider Turning to Your Personal Network If . . .

- You'd like to try out a new idea. You don't need to rely solely on other educators to get feedback on something you're interested in trying in the classroom, especially if you're wondering about student-specific factors such as the interest level of the material.

- You're looking for a way to bring the real world into your classroom. In the fourth edition of *The English Teacher's Companion* (2012), Jim Burke details how he brings community members and parents into his classroom to address topics relevant to his students' studies: when his classes were studying Hamlet, Jim asked parents who are psychiatrists to help students diagnose the troubled prince. After his students wrote resumes, Jim invited the local Rotary Club into his classroom to conduct mock interviews with the students based on their work. The students heard back from the experts—community members who actually make hiring decisions—about their work. What questions or topics in your classroom would benefit from the insights of experts in your network?

Your School Network

Your school network, predictably, is the network you form with your colleagues where you work. Teachers who are connected in their school network help create a culture that "develops teacher leadership explicitly focused on building and sustaining school improvement efforts" (Center for Comprehensive School Reform and Improvement, 2009). Additionally, this report found that participation in a collaborative network "may reduce educator's isolation, foster a shared responsibility for student success, and increase job satisfaction and morale."

Here's a peek at a science department meeting with a group of teachers at Science Leadership Academy, who have created a school-based network for themselves:

Matt: So, how can we give a meaningful presentation opportunity to our ninth-grade students with only a few weeks left in school?

Gamal: What if we had a ninth-grade science fair during the week of June 4th; that way they can share what they have learned?

[Everyone nods and begins speaking at once about different ways to make this happen.]

Gamal: Let me pull up the notes from our last meeting to see if we have anything there to help us with the planning process. I am so excited!

Roz: We could also work on inviting our parents and some folks from the community so the kids have more than just us as their audience.

Have you ever seen a science fair get planned so quickly? And so enthusiastically? You might think I made this example up, but it's true. The teachers on this team trust each other. They know it is safe to dream big, and they are excited to try something new and unexpected. When these teachers come up against a challenge in the classroom or want to try a new idea out, they can bring it to the group and receive feedback. In these meetings, they can refine their ideas; get past their fears and exchange teaching tips. For them, an interaction such as this one removes the barriers between their classrooms. Their collective practice is shared openly so that they can learn from each other.

How Do You Get Started?

If you're just starting at a school (or, better yet, during your interview), ask the leadership team where they see strengths in the faculty. If you're looking to tap into the network in a school where you've been teaching for a while, you could also start with school leaders or teachers on your immediate grade-level or subject-area team. You could also act on the observations you've no doubt made in your time at the school. The art teacher who never seems stressed? The math teacher whose students rush into class and eagerly get to work before the bell rings? These are people who may have some insights or ideas that are worth sharing. The mentors you seek out in your school may also be a perfect place to build a larger school network.

Russ Goerend is a great example of a teacher who has leveraged the support from his colleagues to push his own thinking about his practice and pedagogy.

Russ Goerend

Using a School-Based Network since 2006

Waukee Community School District, Iowa

Profile

My building colleagues make me feel like a professional. We respect each other. That's shown in the ways we're honest and vulnerable with each other. We push each other to think deeply about what's happening in our classrooms. When I first got to this building, I was a new teacher who defaulted to front-of-the-class, teacher-driven instruction. I hoped they learned, and when I was done teaching, we moved on. That quickly changed when I became part of our learning community. We all vowed to make students the center of our rooms, so we dug into learning about the workshop model. Most recently, we all agreed that our use of feedback is lacking, so we're studying that to see how we can do better by our students.

If you're new to the profession, new to a team, or new to a building, use those team-oriented adjectives as your guide: be open, honest, transparent, vulnerable, and humble. Share what's going well. Share what you want to fix. Always view your teammates as fellow professionals who put what's best for all of you and all of your students above whatever ego may potentially get in the way of those vital conversations.

Consider Turning to Your School Network If . . .

- **You're interested in changing the culture of your school.** If you find yourself surrounded by negative or stressful energy at work and want to change things for the better, you can begin by connecting with a few hopeful people and begin a conversation that is solution-oriented. Instead of letting the environment around you defeat your spirit, you can connect with others.

- **You want to reduce stress in your teaching life.** Your colleagues can share classroom management strategies and up-to-date resources with you. Especially if you are teaching a new course or new grade level, a network of other teachers could provide support and reduce your stress as you adjust to new responsibilities. By working together, you can tackle challenges together and learn together rather than going it alone.

- **You want pressing needs addressed by your colleagues.** Your school is providing a professional development session on a new attendance tracker but what you really need help with is how to set up learning centers in your classroom. Your colleagues can suggest concrete strategies to address the challenge you personally face in your classroom. As you seek the solutions that will elevate your practice, you make your own learning relevant for your personal goals—the same kind of focus that we strive to give our students!

- **You want to learn more about your students.** We all have had students in our lives that push the limits of patience. Other teachers who also know your students may be able to give you the context you need to shift your own perspective and to reach these students. Counselors may also be able to paint a more complete picture of your students, anecdotally or with the help of academic records or test scores.

- **You want to make a contribution to your school.** Don't forget the skills and knowledge you bring to a school-based network, too. Are you savvy with technology? Do you have the best bulletin boards in your hallway? Do you always remember to bring banana bread to staff meetings? You also contribute valuable things to your school and colleagues: you are able to give as well as take in a school-based network.

Your Local Network: Edcamp

On a sunny May Saturday morning, I find myself surrounded by at least 175 teachers in the University of Pennsylvania's Wharton School auditorium. There are groups of people who have already found a seat, and others who mill around the door, waiting to find a friendly face in the crowd and find a seat nearby. That day, I attended a session on using Minecraft in the classroom, and, later, another session on using blogs to publish student writing. It was an organic experience: not a single teacher was required to be there or received a stipend for attending. It was truly an example of PD for teachers, by teachers.

Edcamp (edcamp.org) began with a group of teachers in Philadelphia, and the unconference movement has spread across the nation: More than 300 edcamps have been held around the country since its inception in 2010. Edcamps are for teachers who come ready to share their experiences and expertise in a collaborative and interactive learning environment. Often an inquiry or a conundrum drives a day's focus. Edcamp sits in direct contrast to a passive, top-down format of professional development that we often receive in our schools and districts. Instead

Figure 2-1   Session schedule for an edcamp

of waiting to hear what administrators think is important, edcamp attendees and presenters are talking about what they're passionate about in their work.

Before the morning of the edcamp, there is no schedule. Rather, the morning of, participants who would like to present post their sessions on a central schedule display (see Figure 2–1). Any attendee can post a session. The other participants use the display to figure out which sessions to attend. Once the sessions begin, participants join whatever sessions they'd like, and they often vote with their feet and move to another session if they find the one they are in inapplicable to their teaching lives. Not only is this practice accepted, it is encouraged. Learning is the goal at the end of the day: if you're sitting in a session and you are not getting anything relevant from it, no hard feelings, go check out another session. Edcamp spaces are vendor-free so the event is often hosted in a donated space at a school or university.

Consider Joining an Edcamp Network If . . .

- **You're interested in no-cost, high-quality PD.** Let's face it, you didn't get into teaching for the money. Sometimes fees and travel expenses keep you from attending exciting conferences around the country. Edcamp is completely free and free from corporate sponsors. You can attend a local edcamp and be home for dinner if you wanted to.

- **You want to participate and lead, not just sit and get.** Do you like to learn by doing? Do professional development sessions where you are being talked at frustrate you? At a typical edcamp, you have the opportunity to attend sessions based on your interest and if you're not happy with a session, then you can move to another.

- **You want a conference focused on local issues.** Since edcamps emerge when a few local teachers get together and decide to plan one, the issues that are often discussed are based in the local context of a region. You can bring forth issues that affect your school or districts and most likely others in the room will not only relate, but will offer helpful suggestions for change.

- **You want to start practicing your presentations with a low level of stress.** If you have ever wanted to present at a conference but were apprehensive about trying it, you can present at an edcamp. It is a welcoming environment where even first time presenters feel at equal footing with experienced ones. Go out and share the ideas that excite you.

The spontaneity in organization, the serendipitous connections, and the chance to learn from teachers in her local area inspired Mary Beth Hertz, along with a number of fellow educators, to start a movement that has now spread to more than 300 towns and cities across the country.

Mary Beth Hertz

Teaching since 2004/Edcamp Executive Board Secretary

Philadelphia, Pennsylvania

Profile

One of the biggest takeaways edcamp provides for me as far as teaching and learning are concerned is the ability to talk about struggles and dilemmas I have in my classroom and to pick the brains of a variety of educators. For instance, at one edcamp, a teacher was sharing how she uses Symbaloo to organize links for her students. I was not only able to learn about how she used the tool, but also about the thought process that went into how she organized the tiles. This year, as a result of that session, I used Symbaloo to organize sites for my K-2 students and it was highly successful.

I spoke with a new teacher at the recent ISTE conference in San Diego who gushed about her edcamp experience. She was energized by the conversation she experienced and partook in. Edcamp offers new teachers a place to ask questions of veteran teachers, listen in on deep conversations about pedagogy and classroom experiences, build a learning network and realize that it's OK not to have all of the answers.

Your National Networks

National networks can help you tap the knowledge, experience, and power of thousands of educators nationwide.

The National Writing Project

Founded in 1974, National Writing Project (NWP) is a national organization with 70,000 members that promotes writing as well as twenty-first century skills such as digital learning and active participation in the world. It reaches teachers through its nearly 200 university-based project sites around the country, where participants work and learn together on a local level. Despite its name, NWP is not just for teachers of writing. The project welcomes teachers from every content area and grade level (kindergarten through college) who want to develop as writers for their own sake and for the sake of improving writing instruction for their students. Each local project helps teachers of all grades develop as writers through workshops, writing groups, and direct instruction.

As I walk through the door of the Philadelphia Writing Project site, the smell of freshly prepared eggs, bacon, sausage, and pancakes further intensifies my morning hunger. A station for coffee and cartons of juice are set up already. My colleagues are milling about the table. Some have gotten their morning cup of coffee and have already started writing in their morning journals in the conference room.

What follows the morning varies from day to day during the summer institute, but you can expect to be inspired and challenged by what you encounter. After the morning journal, we might turn to a discussion based on an article or try a writing exercise similar to one we may ask our students to take part in. Sometimes we even share our writing aloud (scary, but true).

The institute challenged me to do many of the things we ask our students to do. It helped me to understand the sense of risk and fear that may accompany these activities. I was able to experience what it would feel like to be a student in my own classroom. It was a humbling experience, but it also gave me a lot of ideas for reaching students in my classroom, and raised some important questions: How do we use writing to build communities? How do we form an inquiry community? How do we honor home literacies in school writing communities?

How do you get started/How do you contribute?

To learn more, contact your local site via www.nwp.org. Many sites have initiatives happening throughout the year, so you don't have to wait until the summer institute to get involved.

Luke's experience reminds us how much better and deeper our practice can get when we are in good company. Organizations like NWP encourage teachers to lift the curtain and share the vulnerable experiences we all face every day in the classroom.

Luke Zeller

Teaching English since 2009

Overbrook High School, Philadelphia, Pennsylvania

Profile

NWP made me feel like a professional. I became part of a community of teachers who treated each other like professionals capable of theorizing and understanding our own practice. It gave me inspiration at a crucial time early in my career because my ideals as a young teacher were in danger of being eradicated. I did not always feel supported at my school; I often felt like I was on an island. I was in a process of deprofessionalization and deskilling whereby teaching and learning was being reduced to a process of attempting to transfer skills and knowledge, or what Paulo Freire referred to as the "banking method of education." NWP, specifically PhilWP, encouraged me to focus and develop my teaching skills to pursue transformational classroom practice, rather than relying on reductive instructional strategies.

New teachers should get involved with NWP early and often. When the deskilling of our profession occurs, we need all of the support and guidance we can get in order to pursue authentic teaching.

Consider Joining the National Writing Project If . . .

- **You're interested in joining a community of smart, thoughtful, and engaged teachers.** The common characteristics of NWP teachers tend to be that they are curious, they see themselves as learners and teachers, and they strive to provide great learning experiences for their students. In truth, I was actually a bit intimidated by their brilliance and commitment at first, but I found that they are warm and welcoming. Once you have attended a summer institute, you join a national and local network of teachers who support and encourage each other's work, collaborate on projects, and celebrate each other's successes in the classroom.

- **You're looking for more student-centered ways to teach writing in your classroom.** Instead of arming teachers with boxes of scripted curriculum, NWP will ask you to do exactly the things that you ask your students to do, and to consider your own journey toward becoming a stronger reader and writer. You will be asked to write, publish, and share your work during the summer institute. Now that I've been through the institute, I have a better idea of what my students are feeling when I ask them to write or share, and I write when my students are writing. Letting my students see me learning and struggling as a writer beside them sets a positive tone in the classroom— it reminds them that we are all here to learn.

- **You'd like to find your voice as a writer.** The Digital Is website, created in partnership with the McArthur Foundation, gives members a platform to publish reflections on your practice or even invite your students to share their voices (digitalis.nwp.org). Many NWP teachers have gone on to publish journal articles and books.

National Professional Organizations

In 2011, at the National Council for Teachers of English (NCTE) conference, I found myself in a workshop led by Penny Kittle, Carol Jago, and Judith Ortiz Cofer. On a clean, new page of my journal, I traced the outline of my left hand. Inside these lines, I jotted down my memories of hands—hands that have shaped me, cradled me, molded me, and even hurt me. We had just finished watching Sarah Kay perform her slam poem "Hands" and now it was our turn to use our hands as a memory trigger and begin to write. I was writing about personal memories. Later, I would turn them into a beginning of a creative nonfiction piece. Here are my other notes from this workshop:

> Judith Ortiz Cofer: "language is power, the minute you open your mouth, you reveal yourself. Our students need to find their voices and power within themselves"

Carol Jago: "In a writing conference, the student becomes a fellow writer, you're listening to the text and writer to learn … by nature writer is a listener and observer"

Penny Kittle: "When conferencing with a student, I like to ask questions: Do you like it? Does it represent you well?"

I spent the three days of the conference rushing to sessions, exploring the booths in the exhibit hall, meeting people face-to-face who I'd only known through online connections until then, and preparing for and delivering my own session. These national professional organizations' annual conferences draw thousands—sometimes tens of thousands—of educators, making them some of the most exciting and exhausting professional development that I've ever experienced.

Gamal's connections have helped him nourish a long and successful career as an instructor.

Gamal Sherif

Teaching science since 1993, Member of NSTA since 2006
Philadelphia, Pennsylvania

Profile

NSTA has served as a terrific venue for professional networking. Colleagues and I have co-presented at several NSTA conferences and I enjoy reading NSTA publications. It's been a real joy to explore inquiry-driven science education within the NSTA frame.

My advice for the new teacher is to consider one's professional aims—for the short- and long-term. If a teacher wants to have a profound impact on STEM education, then NSTA serves as an informative clearinghouse for the national discourse—as engaging or mundane, as parts of that discourse may seem. Alternatively, new teachers may be drawn to teacher leadership and advocacy through such organizations as the Center for Teaching Quality, NBPCT, or ASCD.

National professional organizations—often grouped around discipline—allow teachers to share a common subject area or interest. They are often the standard-bearers for specific content areas. Many organizations develop educational standards; issue policy statements; publish journals, newsletter, and books; hold local and regional conferences; and provide solid online resources and rich communities for their members. Some of these benefits are also open to nonmembers as well. These organizations believe in the model of teachers as leaders; amidst the cacophony of education reform debates, they believe teachers should have a seat at the table and a prominent voice when it comes to improving our schools.

How do you get started/How do you contribute?

Many of today's professional organizations have robust websites that are packed with information, ideas, and strong twitter feeds—simply spending some time checking out the organization online can help you to get a feel for it (see Figure 2–2). If you become a member, you'll have the option to receive newsletters, journals, and emails from the organization on topics that are tailored to your content area. Most professional organizations have smaller special interest groups that are open to all members. You might also want to join a local affiliate in your area to start connecting with teachers closer to you.

Figure 2-2 Major national professional organizations

There is a national professional organization for every subject area and area of interest to teachers. Here's a quick list of a few of the largest organizations:

National Council of Teachers of English (NCTE)
www.ncte.org (annual member dues: $50.00)

National Council of Teachers of Mathematics (NCTM)
www.nctm.org (annual member dues: $81.00)

National Science Teachers Association (NSTA)
www.nsta.org (annual member dues: $75.00)

National Council for the Social Studies (NCSS)
www.socialstudies.org
(annual member dues: $79.00)

Teachers of English to Speakers of
Other Languages (TESOL)
www.tesol.org (annual member dues: $95.00)

International Society for Technology in
Education (ISTE)
www.iste.org (annual member dues: $39–$212)

International Reading Association (IRA)
www.reading.org (annual member dues: $39.00)

National Association for the Education of
Young Children (NAEYC)
www.naeyc.org (annual member dues vary by
affiliate group location)

National Association for Bilingual Education (NABE)
www.nabe.org (annual member dues: $60.00)

ASCD (formerly the Association for Supervision and
Curriculum Development)
www.ascd.org (annual member dues: $59.00)

The Association of Teacher Educators
www.ate1.org (annual member dues: $100)

Consider Joining a National Professional Organization If . . .

- **You're interested in being part of a professional community in your subject area.** Joining the national professional organization devoted to teaching your subject area feeds both your love of content and your dedication to your students.

- **You're interested in furthering your own learning.** Consider joining a professional organization if you're looking for a larger community of teachers who believe in the power of good instruction to make a difference in the lives of our students. If you enjoy learning new things about teaching, and you see your own learning tied to your students' learning, you will find invaluable resources via their sites, list-serves and online courses, and professional development sessions.

- **You are looking to get the word out about your work.** Are you innovative in the classroom? Do you use technology in an interesting and thoughtful way with your students? Do you conduct teacher research in your classroom? If you said yes to any of these questions, then these organizations are certainly eager to hear from you. A professional organization for teachers can help you get the word out about your work via their communications networks, their conferences, and even their publishing divisions.

- **You are looking for ways to connect to teachers from outside of your region.** Want to see your classroom from the other side of the country? Want to gain a wider perspective on your practice and profession? Then joining a professional organization can take you out of the doldrums of everyday routine and allow you to see things anew. As Proust said, "The real voyage of discovery consists not in seeking new landscapes but in having new eyes."

- **You need help articulating the best practices you're using in your classroom.** A professional organization for teachers can provide you with research and weight for the thoughtful approaches you use toward teaching your students. If these practices are ever questioned or being challenged, you can turn to the resources provided by a professional organization to help you articulate the benefits of your practice.

- **You feel disappointed or discouraged by political discourse around teachers and want to take a stand.** As the saying goes, if you're not angry then you're not paying attention. From Madison, WI to Philadelphia, PA to Miami, FL, teachers are under attack. We have become a country that sees teachers as the fat cats of society. If you want to weather this storm or even stand up against it, join your colleagues in a professional organization to take a collective political stance.

Your Web-based Network

Web-based communities are online spaces that give teachers a chance to exchange ideas, solutions, and inquiries, fostering teacher leadership and creativity. Some teachers write regularly about their practice and post it on blogs. You can visit the blogs or subscribe to them via a RSS reader. Often times, the best conversations take place in the comments where other readers may raise questions or concerns based on the original author's post. You will discover more blogs as these bloggers will often link to other blogs that they regularly read. Don't worry about trying to read everything! You'll learn from whatever you find time to read.

I have found web-based networking particularly helpful this year because I am teaching eleventh grade for the first time. This is also my first year at a new school, and I am going to be teaching Arthur Miller's *The Crucible* for the first time. As I do for every new unit, book, or idea I am trying out, I start by doing a search in the threads of English Companion Ning. I also send a tweet out asking for help, ideas—anything, really. I find out that Dana Huff, a fellow English teacher and Twitter friend has some great introduction activities for a *Crucible* unit. Even though I am daunted by the task of writing a new unit plan while finishing up an old one and grading many papers at the same time, I know that I have connections through the Internet that can help me to find valuable, applicable resources quickly. Some of the resources I've found include a WebQuest introducing the background of the play, a detailed character list map, and guide to reproducing the scenes from the play in the classroom. These resources have not only saved me precious time to work with my students but they have also given me an opportunity to deepen my practice and fine-tune my instruction.

An Example of a Thriving Online Community For Teachers: The English Companion Ning

The English Companion Ning (englishcompanion.ning.com) pulls together English teachers from around the country with various levels of experience who want to share their practice and learn from others. Essentially, it is a message board: if you have a question about a book, a procedure, or a unit plan, you simply post a question and you will receive responses from other teachers, often with links or attached documents which answer your question. Or, if you see that someone is asking a question that you think you can help with, you can post your own answer or resources. While there wasn't a site like the EC Ning in the areas of Science, Math, and Social Studies when this book went to press, I'm hopeful that there will be in the future—perhaps you can take the initiative to create one of these.

Figure 2–3 is an example of the help I found while I was looking for resources for my *The Crucible* unit.

Figure 2–3   A typical discussion on English Companion Ning: Screenshot July 14, 2012

Replies to This Discussion

 ∞ Reply by Carol S on Tuesday

I use most of these in my chronological AmerLit study. A couple that I would add/substitute:
Edward Taylor's "Meditation Six" compares us to money. We are God's gold. My students really respond to this.
Ben Franklin's "Epitaph"   which compares the body to a book--"revised and edited by the Author." I then have the kids write their own metaphorical epitaphs.

Definitely show the film of *The Crucible* with Daniel Day-Lewis as Proctor and Wynona Ryder as Abigail. Good stuff.

For resources material, take a look at Shmoop and at 60 Second Recap .   Both these links take you to material on *The Crucible*, but both sites have oodles of titles.

► Reply   ✉ Message

 ∞ Reply by Kati Kapral on Tuesday

Thank you so much for your reply. I had planned on using the Daniel day-Lewis/Wynona Ryder film to accompany the play. I responded well to that film when I was a student. I will also read the other two works that you mentioned. I'm reading articles, forums, supplementary material, and taking as many notes as I can to prepare for my first year teaching! I'm reaching a point where I've prepared as much as I can to this point and might just have to learn as I go from here. Do you have any advice or suggestions about American Literature as a whole? What worked in the past & what really didn't?

► Reply

 ∞ Reply by Kathryn Gazso on Wednesday

Kati I'm going back to teaching American Lit after quite a few years off -- it's exciting! What I remember from the last time is this -- my students breathed a sigh a

Teachers like Meredith are able to overcome challenges because they aren't afraid to ask for help and they know how to plug into networks like the EC Ning and leverage it to find solutions for their classroom challenges.

Profile

Meredith Stewart

Teaching since 2008, Member of EC Ning since 2010
Raleigh-Durham, North Carolina

I came to the Ning primarily because I felt that I'd gotten myself in over my head. I was in my first full-time teaching position and felt in serious need of mentoring and ideas for teaching Language Arts since it wasn't my primary area of focus in college and graduate school. On the Ning, I found experienced teachers and experts in the field who were willing to answer my questions, offer suggestions for challenges I encountered, and suggest ideas for lessons. It became my lifeline for that first year of teaching English. My relationships on the Ning have grown into friendships with some of the members as we've worked on projects, edited each other's articles, and presented at conferences together.

The EC Ning has grown over the years, but new teachers shouldn't be afraid to jump in. First, search for threads that deal with the topic that you're interested in, and if you don't see it addressed, create a new thread. If someone doesn't respond to you right away, don't get discouraged; be patient and persistent. Also, seek out ways to contribute your knowledge to the Ning. Don't think that just because you're new that you don't have valuable ideas to contribute.

How do you get started with Ning?

On Ning, it is easier to build and nurture your connections than in other online forums. When faced with a question about your practice, you can post a question and other users can respond to your query. It is ideal for you to post responses, as well, if you have resources that can aide another teacher. Nonetheless, until you feel comfortable, it is okay to lurk here as well.

Twitter

The ever-growing micro-blogging site, Twitter, allows users to post updates, questions, observations, and links on the web in 140 characters or less. It also allows anyone who is interested to read what others are posting. The character limit forces you to post short and effective messages to those who are following your account.

To follow someone means to simply receive tweets she sends out. When someone follows you, whatever you post will be received by anyone who follows your account. The value of this tool comes through in the use of hashtags, a notation that begins with a # and works a bit like an indexing tag. So, for example, if you are tweeting about teaching English, you might use the hashtag, *#engchat*. People who are interested in teaching English can follow that hashtag and see all of the tweets that use that hashtag. This allows small-niche communities to emerge based on similar interests, even if the users don't know each other in any other context. With short, rapid responses, you can post a question or ask for a resource. More than likely, someone on your Twitter stream already has access to these things and will share it with you.

Here is a sampling of tweets from the last few minutes of an #engchat (English chat) that discussed issues of privilege and race. The full transcript of the hour-long chat included many more tweets and overlapping conversations.

e terms preceded by @ are itter handles. Each handle is a er's unique name on Twitter.

is user is responding to _pahomov's question. Starting e tweet with another user's ndle signifies a reply.

Larissa Pahomov @Lpahomov

I also wonder: if your community is coming from a place of privilege, is it harder to initiate these conversations? #engchat

Ann Leaness @aleaness

@Lpahomov visuals help. Real life. Like this http://t.co /KpqhcxyEvP #engchat

Larissa Pahomov @Lpahomov

@aleaness more things like that, please #engchat

@Lpahomov, the moderator for this chat, poses a question to continue the conversation and to spark discussion among participants.

Using this hashtag links these tweets into a conversation. Every tweet in this discussion includes this hashtag.

Tweetchats can be a great place to share resources, as @aleaness does here.

Ann Leaness @aleaness

@Lpahomov I am going to use that as a parallel to Absolute True Diary for jumping off on research with tenth grade. #engchat

Larissa Pahomov @Lpahomov

Okay, the last few minutes of this #engchat is devoted to tips, tricks, or lingering questions you have! #engchat

Rhiannon Maton @RhiannonMaton

@aleaness @Lpahomov Why do students say "we're tired of talking about race"? Where is this coming from? #engchat

Larissa Pahomov @Lpahomov

My tip—I have students look through "critical lenses" by literally putting on big funny sunglasses. Makes it less intimidating. #engchat

Meenoo Rami @meenoorami

I am wondering if you're doing some interesting work around social justice in your class. Pls share what you're working on. #engchat

Larissa Pahomov @Lpahomov

@RhiannonMaton Ss in Philly do a year of African American history. After that, sometimes they're convinced they've covered it all. #engchat

sally_oh_brien @sally_oh_brien

@aleaness @sriii2000 @Lpahomov Yeah, I've seen Ss throw that word out just to throw teachers off their square. #engchat

Ann Leaness @aleaness

@sally_oh_brien @sriii2000 @Lpahomov Yes, then they get serious. #engchat

sally_oh_brien sally_oh_brien

@aleaness @sriii2000 @Lpahomov Right, it's like a test to see if you can actually handle having a real conversation about race. #engchat

Rhiannon Maton @RhiannonMaton

@Lpahomov Thanks. I wonder if there's a different way of framing convos about race then. Need to get kids to connect in new way. #engchat

Ann Leaness @aleaness

@LisaStoneman @RhiannonMaton @Lpahomov Yes. Mine too sometimes. #engchat

Larissa Pahomov @Lpahomov

Okay, it's 8pm and that marks an official close to this week's #engchat! Thanks to everybody for the thoughts and resources.

Meenoo Rami @meenoorami

Huge thanks to @Lpahomov and @TAGPhilly for getting us together tonight in Philly and on the web. #engchat Thanks to everyone who joined us!

Ann Leaness @aleaness

@sally_oh_brien @sriii2000 @Lpahomov I think part of it is because we were taught to not talk about race, upsets the apple cart. #engchat

Ann Leaness @aleaness

RT @@meenoorami: Huge thanks to @Lpahomov and @TAGPhilly for getting us together tonight in Philly and on the web. #engchat Thanks to everyo…

ere, @aleaness retweeted mething from @meenoorami e!)--she re-sent my tweet out her followers.

Larissa Pahomov @Lpahomov

If you're in Philadelphia (or anywhere, really) you can find great current ed and SJ info at http://t.co/ERwMnsHCos #engchat

Seecantrill @Seecantrill

Great questions @Lpahomov great convo #engchat Night!

It's fine to simply be polite in a tweetchat—you don't have to say something profound!

Conversations often continue beyond the chat times, and new conversations pop up during the week between chats. While the appointed chat time is the best time to join a big conversation, people use the hashtag to reach out to others all the time.

Larissa Pahomov @Lpahomov

@aleaness I think, then, that acknowledging that teaching is an important step #engchat

Ann Leaness @aleaness

Thanks @Lpahomov and @@meenoorami for a great conversation. #engchat

Here, I'm letting people know when the next #engchat will be and what we'll be discussing. I ask people to retweet to get the word out.

Meenoo Rami @meenoorami

#engchat w/ @thereadingzone—Celebrating National Day on Writing #write2connect. Pls RT.

Oct. 21 at 7 PM ET

Tweetchats can move quickly: All of the above tweets (and many more—too many to include in this book!) were posted in just a few minutes. Participants often find themselves scrolling back through the chat archives later to find conversation threads that they missed.

While the fast-paced discussion of Twitter chats can be overwhelming at first, participants usually leave the discussion with an array of resources on a given topic. When starting out, do not feel the pressure to keep up with the chat, do your best to chime in if you want. There many members of these tribes who do not even make it to the scheduled chat times but will peruse the archives later at a more convenient time.

How do you get started with Twitter?

You can begin by getting a twitter account. You might want to start with following some people you already know. Many authors of professional books for teachers and influential educators are tweeting regularly. You can also check to see who they follow to continue to extend your circle. One thing to remember here is that at first, you may choose to only lurk and not post any tweets of your own. That is completely okay. The more you interact with other people by replying to their tweets, the larger and stronger your connections in this network will be. You can also post questions and ask others to retweet your request to reach a larger audience. Twitter is an intuitive tool but it does take some time to build a network so don't get discouraged.

Joining scheduled conversations with other teachers can help you interact with people in real time and meet new people to follow. Here's a quick list of some of the most popular chats, including #engchat, the discussion group I founded in 2010.

Shelley Krause @butwait

Twitter is my laboratory, faculty lounge, news wire, librarian, crystal ball, tech conf., art project, classroom, dinner party… #satchat

8:18 am—8/24/2013

- **English:** #engchat, every Monday at 7 PM EST

- **Social Studies:** #sschat, every Monday at 7 PM EST

- **Math:** #mathchat, every Thursday at 8 PM EST

- **Science:** #scichat, every Tuesday at 8 PM EST

For a full list of all Twitter educational chats, check out http://goo.gl/WS7Zo from Jerry Blumengarten or scan the QR code. Finally, checking out the links in tweets will often lead you to blogs about education. As you get to know the blogs and their authors' voices, you may find that there are some that you'd like to check out regularly.

Consider Joining a Web-Based Community If . . .

- **You're interested in getting just-in-time professional development.** It's great to go to conferences or even join a webinar when you have time, but what about when you need help Sunday night figuring out the best way to teach your students about diffusion and osmosis? Well, this is the moment where you can tap into a vast network of colleagues and ask for help. This is professional development when you need it, tailored completely to your needs.

- **You want a wider perspective on your practice.** You don't have to wait to attend a conference to gain a wider perspective on your practice. Write a blog post. Exchange emails. Tweet out a picture of student work in your classroom. Let others see what you're doing and probe them to think on it, get feedback and continue to refine your work with your students.

- **You want to connect your students to students from different places, cultures, and backgrounds.** The best work we do with students is real world; it isn't about playing school with our students. The work we assign them and the work we do alongside them should be connected to their experience in the world. By connecting with teachers from around the world, you will be able to connect your students to new experiences, ideas, cultures, and people.

- **You want to connect directly to experts. Web-based communities can help you make contact with experts.** Are you impressed with a professional book you've read recently? Chances are you can find the author on Twitter and strike up a conversation. With use of Google video chat and Skype you can bring experts, authors, and innovators directly into your classroom. Teaching your students about the stock market or advertising? Connect your students with a broker or a creative director from an agency and try out their ideas and learn from industry leaders.

Yeah, But . . .

There are many reasons we resist the idea of becoming connected or networking. For some of us it is the fear of rejection, for others it is the feeling of being pressed for time and not wanting to add another commitment to our lives. Here are the most common reasons teachers may resist the idea of being connected and why they should overcome such resistance:

- **I am just too busy.** Teachers are challenged enough just striking a balance between their personal and professional lives and asking them to invest more time in building and sustaining a network may seem like an unreasonable burden. Nonetheless, a robust and responsive network can help you save time and energy in planning and finding innovative solutions to your everyday quandaries from the classroom.

- **I just want to do my own thing.** Some of us like the autonomy that comes with our classroom life; we can choose to close the door and live in our little corner of the world. However, when we do this, we take away the chance for us to learn from others near and far from us. Plus, if we want our students to be collaborative problem-solvers that our increasingly complex world requires, we must model this mode of learning for them.

- **I don't really see results from networking.** Some of us get impatient with our networking efforts; it takes a while to build a collaborative network. For example, it may be difficult to see the point of Twitter when you have few followers and hardly anyone responds to your requests. However, with patience and reciprocity, you can slowly build a network where there is mutual exchange of support. It may be hard to see the benefits of putting the time in creating a network but they are well worth it in the end.

Moving Forward

We live and teach in the most challenging *and* exciting times for our nation. On one hand, we are facing massive dropout rates (1.3 million high school students per year) and sliding back on our Math and Science performance in comparison to other countries (#17 in the world) (The Broad Foundation). On the other hand, we are at the precipice of a tipping point in revolutionizing education. There is an underground swell of teachers who want to move away from the factory model of education to education for the next generation of change-agents, from teachers as sages to teachers as co-learners. The challenges that our students will inherit in the forms of poverty, global warming, access to clean water, and wars are going to require empathy, innovation, and creativity. These qualities cannot be tested on a bubble sheet. We must give our students a chance to practice solving complex problems collaboratively so that they are prepared to do so when they leave our classrooms behind.

Our nation rightfully expects us to prepare the next generation of writers, thinkers, inventors, and leaders. To do our level best with this responsibility, we need to connect as a community of teachers on the local, national, and international level to share best practices and support our students' learning. Just like our students, we need to form rich connections to colleagues near and far to make our own learning meaningful.

CHAPTER 3

Keep Your Work Intellectually Challenging

First, the subjects we teach are as large and complex as life, so our knowledge of them is always flawed and partial. No matter how we devote ourselves to reading and research, teaching requires a command of content that always eludes our grasp. Second, the students we teach are larger than life and even more complex. To see them clearly and see them whole, and respond to them wisely in the moment, requires a fusion of Freud and Solomon that few of us achieve.

—Parker J. Palmer, *The Heart of a Teacher*

If you are a new teacher, especially if you are passionate about the intellectual joys of your subject matter, you may have found the realities of teaching a bit shocking. After all, when you decided to become a teacher, you may have imagined a classroom of highly engaged students who would love your discipline as much as you do. It's the dream, right? However, the thrill of landing a teaching job is often soon replaced with a harsh adjustment of your expectations when you see the work that is actually set in front of you: stacks of rules, regulations, and requirements, and students who have little interest or experience in your subject area. And after you have actually figured out how to use your school's attendance system, how to keep the peace during your shift on lunch duty, how to report your grades in the required format, and a thousand other things that have nothing to do with your subject matter, you might begin to wonder if teaching is really an intellectual job after all. I hope you have realized the answer: yes. It's just a different intellectual challenge than many of us anticipate.

At Science Leadership Academy, I teach a twelfth-grade class second semester called Storytelling, which is a hybrid study of master storytellers and creative writing. By the time many students enter twelfth grade, they have mastered the art of argument but have lost their zeal for creating characters, situations, and dialogue along the way. In my class, we go back to finding joy in writing. Usually, I ask students to write about their identity as readers and writers to help me get to know those students I may not have taught in the previous year. While this task helped me to get to know my students deeply, it did nothing to build a community of readers and writers in the class at the beginning of the semester. Since students lacked the necessary trust with each other, they were reluctant to share their writing and give each other feedback. I tried to think of different ways to address this lack of trust. How could I help them see each other as storytellers?

I thought about that question throughout the year as I went about my teaching, reading, and networking. This year when I taught that unit, I made what looked like a split-second decision that changed the way the rest of the semester worked out. The first day, I gave them this assignment: perform a mini story slam, where you tell a story, without notes, for three to five minutes in front of your classmates. The stories ranged from humorous incidents to things my students had never shared with their peers. Their honesty, vulnerability, and willingness to truly listen to each other's stories created an environment where they felt more at ease with sharing their work during the rest of the semester. For my students, the change in the assignment wasn't monumental in terms of action. However, this act of sharing created the necessary trust within our writing community. As a result, that decision I made had a tremendous impact on how the rest of the semester played out in our classroom community.

As teachers, we make game time decisions all the time, and often overlook the complexity of those choices because we are too busy to do otherwise. Good and Brophy (2008) write that teachers face 1,000 decision points per day. While this constant decision making can wear us down, it also gives us a chance to recognize the power that lies within our ability to choose. We hold the ability to redirect the course of learning in our classroom at any given second. When we own our ability to create conditions where learning and joy can live side by side, we take the power back.

The internal dialogue and decision making process our minds go through while teaching reveal our ability to make key decisions that change learning outcomes for our students. We need to honor the complexity that lives in the art of teaching. These seemingly simple decisions are often based on weighing complex factors that make up our work as teachers, including temperament of certain students, the time of the year, time allotted for this unit, size of the class, and past experiences with these specific groups of students. This intellectual challenge trumps any paper I wrote on Hegel's dialectical movement in college. It's also what keeps me coming back to the classroom year after year.

The Importance of Naming Our Complexity

In many ways, it's hard to imagine a field that requires the mix of intellect, passion, and game-time decisions that teaching does. Ron Brandt characterized teachers as the "managers of complexity" (1986, 5), and if we reflect on our daily work of delivering and differentiating a lesson to our students, it seems like an apt label. The key is we take this swirl of information and take action. As the Concordia University "Teacher Education Conceptual Framework" articulates:

> The skills needed to manage complexity often boil down to decision making. The complexities of instruction, teacher-student relations, student-student relation, parental interactions, and administrative expectations all come to bear upon the daily actions of the teacher, and those complexities require appropriate decision making.

While all the complexities of decision making seem burdensome, the findings of Rosabeth Moss Kanter, professor at Harvard Business School, suggests that meeting these challenges gives us an opportunity for happiness. In writing her book *Evolve! Succeeding in the Digital Culture of Tomorrow* (2001), she discovered:

> The happiest people I know are dedicated to dealing with the most difficult problems. Turning around inner city schools. Finding solutions to homelessness or unsafe drinking water. Supporting children with terminal illnesses. They face the seemingly worst of the world with a conviction that they can do something about it and serve others. (2013)

Standing up in front of thirty-three sleepy teenagers on Monday morning and exalting the beauty of Shakespeare (or linear equations, chemical reactions, or mercantilism) takes some serious guts. Getting a student who reads significantly below his grade level to not only comprehend *The Odyssey* but also connect the pangs of Telemachus who is missing an absent father to his own life is a worthy challenge. You don't think about the complex factors at work or all of the cognitive decisions in those early morning epiphanies. Instead, you see beauty, joy, challenge, and purpose in any of those concepts that you teach, and you hope to ignite the same passion in your students. But recognizing the complexity of what we do each day can be a way to energize and empower our work.

Our sense of fulfillment as teachers begins and ends with knowing that we are tackling one of the most pressing questions of our time: How do we prepare our students to tackle the complex challenges our world faces? Our multifarious work of teaching, trying to find new ways to reach our students, continues to provide us with joy and a sense of accomplishment.

How Do We Maintain Our Motivation?

I am sure you have had those moments in your classroom where your students are completely engaged in the process of learning, where magic happens in surprising ways. Mihaly Csikszentmihalyi's identifies this immersion in a task as "flow," which he describes as "a sense of merging with the activity" (2000). It's what we imagine will happen when we enter our classroom in the first place. However, with the disruptions and demands on our work, it can be hard to maintain. Csikszentmihalyi's research explains that people can find that flow if they have "very high levels of intrinsic motivation . . . marked by . . . strong interest and involvement in the work" (2000). Our challenge is to figure out how to do this in our daily work of teaching.

According to author Daniel Pink, when dealing with work that is complex and that requires creativity—basically, work like ours—people need three things to feel motivated: autonomy, mastery, and purpose. The more that you strive to bring these three factors under your control, the more likely you are to have the strong internal motivation that you need to drive your work (2009).

Autonomy

In this time of public scrutiny of education, it's not uncommon for teachers to feel that they need permission to act in large and small ways: to reframe curriculum to meet the needs of students, to apply for grants for things needed in the classroom, or permission to organize an event for parents in the community. When we don't get that permission, it chips away at our sense of autonomy. But remember that we are the experts of our craft. While we know to keep an open mind toward ideas from colleagues, parents, and administration, we must not let outside input paralyze our own sound judgment about what is good for our kids.

Another unintended consequence of loss of autonomy is how it makes us stagnant as teachers; it brings the evolution of our teaching practice to a disheartening halt. Instead of moving forward on challenges that we can address, we may find ourselves doing nothing at all. This is probably the worst consequence of disempowerment of educators in our times.

Without autonomy, work can feel like nothing more than drudgery. As Csikszentmihalyi explains, "when we feel that we are investing attention in a task against our will, it is as if our psychic energy is being wasted. Instead of helping us to reach our own goals, it is called upon to make someone else's dream come true" (2008, 160). Often, the struggle for autonomy isn't always based on external factors or permissions. Often, our doubts hold us back from taking our own ideas seriously and implementing them. If you struggle with these doubts, consider these questions:

- When have you felt that you could act autonomously in your work in the past school year?

- When have you felt that you needed permission from others?

- When did your hesitation keep you from seizing a great opportunity for your students?

Mastery

In our work, mastery does not mean perfection: we are not programming droids, but rather we play an essential role in shaping the learning lives of young people. However, it does mean we must continue the deliberate act of reflection on our actions and relentlessly pursue improvement. We will never reach a fulfilling end point in our work because our craft will continue to evolve. Each year, we meet a new set of students who will teach us things as well. Sarah Brown Wessling, 2010 National Teacher of the Year, put it best, "I have horrible lessons too. Of course I do. . . . Every variety of failure and misstep: I've done it. But I'm not afraid of mistakes and I'm not ashamed of them. I learn and tweak and grow and get better, not because I was ever perfect to begin with, but because I am compelled to get it right . . . eventually" (2013). In this constant pursuit, we hone our art. As you begin the year, you may want to consider these questions, discuss them with your colleagues, and even set a few goals as a way to keep them on your radar throughout your daily life of teaching:

- What am I trying to master this year? How am I challenging myself?

- What will make me feel stronger for having accomplished this year?

- How am I finding intellectual joy in the work that I am doing this year?

Purpose

Unlike other careers where a worker might wonder how selling her quota of widgets makes the world a better place, we already know. It's one of the best parts of being a teacher. We have a clear purpose. When we stay at school past 7 pm on a Friday night, we don't wonder why we are doing the work. We understand that the work we do matters because we see the future problem-solvers, tinkerers, and innovators of our country each day in our classroom. We understand our problems—war, poverty, and climate change—are in the hands of our students and they will have the power to change the course of our fate as humanity. We work to prepare them to meet that challenge.

- What is the work, the goal, the project, or the student that gives you purpose?
- When have you not been able to keep purpose at the forefront of your work with students?
- At what point in the day/year is your purpose crystal clear to you? When is it hard to grasp?

When we view our work through the lenses of gaining autonomy, working toward mastery, and recognizing the true purpose of our work, we jump-start our own intrinsic motivation and open ourselves to master the intellectual challenges that we will face continuously in our daily work.

Autonomy, Mastery, and Purpose in Action

On the night before grades are due, or the day that you have cafeteria duty, it might be difficult to remember that, ultimately, we have the power to make our work intellectually challenging, but that responsibility always rests with us. How can we find intellectual joy in our work?

Reframe Our Work

The first step we can take in valuing the intellectual challenges in our work is changing our perspective. It may mean shifting our vision of intellectual work from the content-specific work we might have done as undergrads to the challenging, student-focused work that is at the heart of our profession—without ever losing our love of our content areas. The name of the game is balance—the managing of constant tensions between content and student-driven pedagogical decisions (Figure 3–1). Feeling empowered to balance these tensions in your classroom makes us better teachers in the end.

Figure 3–1 What do we believe?

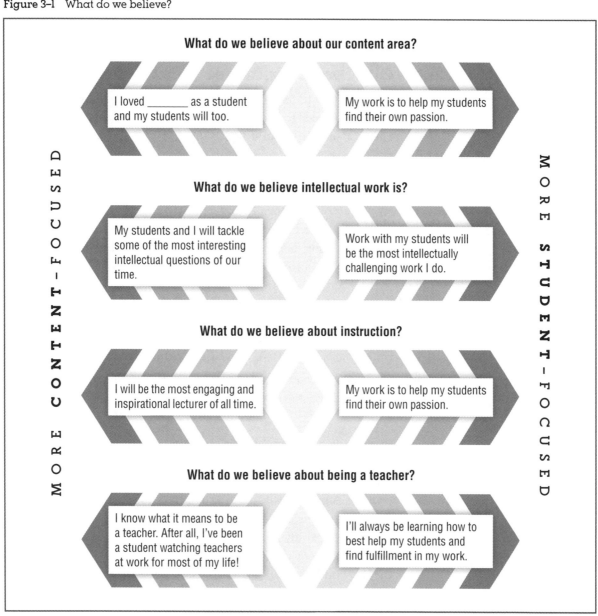

In each of these shifts, the mind pivots from individual responsibility to a collaborative stance on a teacher's practice. These new shifts involve seeing a classroom as a complex network of stakeholders—teacher, students, parents, administration, and community members—all who want to see your students succeed. A teacher can leverage these connections to solve complex problems facing the school community. Embracing this challenge is not only an incredible intellectual challenge, it is also an emotional and ethical challenge that emphasizes the purpose of your work and your own autonomy.

Create Our Own Curriculum

In teaching, we are asked to teach vast amounts of content and life-long skills and habits our students will need to become active citizens and members of our society. This task is no easy one. In a world history class, it could mean uncovering the human history from prehistoric times to present day. In math and science classes, basic concepts of things that make up the universe and our bodies are discovered. We simply cannot manage this task without having a good grasp of what we're teaching, why we're teaching it, and what sequence we will follow. Framing your curriculum in some ways is like rolling out a vision and a mission for a group of talented people and getting them onboard so that you can begin meaningful work.

Many teachers are daunted by the task of writing curriculum and feel like it is an arduous task in addition to time-consuming work such as grading, preparing lessons, and communicating with students and parents. Often times, teachers are handed prepackaged curriculum when they begin work in a new school. It can be tempting to rely on curriculum that has been developed by "experts"—both because of the persuasive marketing on those products and the hope of saving some precious time. However, when we decide to use a prewritten curriculum, we are not only letting go of our autonomy and turning down an authentic intellectual challenge, we are also short-changing our students.

Prepackaged curriculum assumes that all of your students are identical learners. Because you spend time at the beginning of the year learning about the interests, strengths, and home lives of your students, you know that you're not teaching a homogeneous caricature of a student in your class. Zaria has a deep interest and knowledge of graphic novels, while Maria would have a hard time getting through a single one. While some ready-made curriculum claims to include differentiation, it is often lacking in substance. Publishers of curriculum assume that all students learn the same way and have the same interests, but you know that this just isn't true. Your students would benefit much more from having you tailor their learning goals, plans, and assessment to match their individual interests and strengths.

Prepackaged curriculum does not address students' needs. It assumes that you can put a student in front of a reading program or learn remedial math for a couple of hours and spark a love for either reading or solving problems.

Prepackaged curriculum isn't necessarily written or reviewed by experts. Many textbook programs label themselves as research-based and even hire high-profile authors. Educational researcher and author Peter Dewitz has interviewed people who make textbooks—authors, publishers, and editors—and he has found that the process of making prepackaged curriculum does not inspire confidence in the programs:

> The lessons, workbooks, and assessment tools are largely subcontracted to development houses. The authors of the program rarely review any of this work; . . . much has to be written by many different people, with little time for review by the authors of the program. . . . Ultimately there is the compromise between what the research recommends and what the educational marketplace demands. (Dewitz and Wolskee 2012, 9–10)

Prepackaged curriculum doesn't prepare students for real-world challenges. As Daniels and Zemelman point out in *Subjects Matter*, textbooks are "exceedingly hard to read" (2004, 40)—long, dry, and loaded with facts and terminology unlike any form of text that students are likely to encounter in the outside world. When we rely on the textbook as the main source of knowledge, "We virtually pretend that textbooks aren't reference books at all—but rather some strange hybrid text form: long, fact-packed stories that a person can read day in and day out, memorizing with fascination, and passing statewide tests upon completion" (40–41).

Curriculum planning for your students is like planning meals for your family. A home-made meal with quality ingredients always trumps fast food, and it presents new and interesting intellectual challenges for the chef.

There is no denying it: creating student-centered, culturally-relevant, and engaging curriculum for your students is no small task, but is more rewarding to you and your students than faithfully following a prepackaged program. Initially, it can be more work, but the rewards are bigger too. Will every unit you plan be perfect? No, but you may learn more from the units that don't fully work for your students than the ones that do. Kira Baker-Doyle worked with a group of teachers from Upper Dublin High School to help them create their own curriculum and her reflections show the power of a group of teachers coming together to build a curriculum that meets the needs of their students.

> At Upper Dublin High School we have a collaborative professional development group called the Upper Dublin-Arcadia Teacher Collaborative (UDATC). We meet every week to talk about our teaching, share experiments, and explore new ideas. What makes us unique is that we are not just Upper Dublin teachers—we are student teachers, faculty from Arcadia, former students, and school leaders. We bring many different perspectives to the work, which generates new ways of thinking and builds respect for others' situations or beliefs. We do share certain guiding principles as a group—that we are learners with our students, that the students are at the center, and that we need to connect learning experiences with the world at large. These ideas guide us and make us ask questions about our work, ultimately helping us to take risks and innovate in a sustainable way. As one teacher put it, "if you fail alone it feels like failure and you want to give up, but if you try something and fail with UDATC, it just makes you think, 'what can I do differently next time?'"

But what if I am required to use prepackaged curriculum? If you find yourself in the position that you are required to use prepackaged curriculum, consider how to balance it by incorporating the authentic inquiry that your students bring to your classroom. For example:

- In an Environmental Science class, invite your local government representative to answer questions prepared by your students regarding how local policy is impacting local ecology.

- In a Statistics class, see if your students can present their analysis of local use of public spaces to city/town planners in your area.

- In an American government class, have your students develop students' Bill of Rights for your class, school, or district.

These are just a few simple ideas to add depth and inquiry to a curriculum that you are handed, where you're trying to bring authentic student choices and inquiry to the classroom.

Read Widely in Your Profession

Constantly challenging yourself with new ideas and insights can help you look at your own work with fresh eyes and can give you ideas that will help you work toward mastery in your classroom. You might be saying to yourself, who has time for all this? I can barely get through the student work I take home every night and bring back ungraded the next day. It's true that reading in your fields—both your content area and in the field of education—can take time. However, an up-to-date knowledge of best practice in your profession can help you to do your best work and make you feel connected and energized. A few places to get started:

Professional books

Professional books have the power to make us feel less alone on our journey toward improving our practice. By reading these books, I have personally found a new way to reimagine my work with students, get practical advice on classroom challenges, and set new goals for the future. If you're still learning about the range of voices in the professional book world, see the bibliography at the end of this book for a variety of excellent resources.

Journals

Every subject area professional organization offers a journal for subscription to its members. Oftentimes, these journal subscriptions are offered as part of the organization's membership. Take advantage and look through them when you get a chance—they often include cutting-edge research and responses to current issues in the field. Sometimes, I will search the archives of journals available to me online before planning a unit as I often find that journal articles are well researched and offer a host of lesson planning ideas. You may even find a topic that will help you connect to and collaborate with other professionals if you take a moment to glance at the latest issue from a journal in your subject area. I find great ideas for the classroom in the poetry, off the shelves, and teacher-to-teacher sections in the *English Journal* from the National Council of Teachers of English.

Blogs

While journals may come quarterly or monthly from your professional organizations, subject area blogs and Google Plus communities are updated around the clock. I subscribe to and read relevant blogs from thought leaders in my subject area and will often get a new idea from following their class' work online. Not sure what to do for National Poetry Month? Want to find a new way to celebrate Pi Day

(March 14th)? Turn to a blog run by an expert subject area teacher and take away applicable insights for your practice. Be sure to leave comments and engage the blogger, it helps them keep going!

Because new blogs pop up every day, any list of blogs that I include in this book will be out-of-date before long.

Once you start reading blogs regularly, you'll notice comments and links that will lead you to new voices. If you're following people in your fields on Twitter, you will also find links to blogs.

Videos

Easy access to video has transformed our profession in the last few years. Teachers can easily capture their work in the classroom and review it for personal and professional growth. Organizations such as Teaching Channel and National Board for Professional Teaching Standards are using video to not only reflect on teaching practice but also improve teacher performance in the classroom. You can find many high-quality videos on the web to peek a glance at another colleague's classroom nearby or across the country.

Do the Reading You Enjoy

When strapped for time and feeling inundated with the amount of work you're doing for your classes, the thought of just enjoying the Sunday *New York Times* or the latest collection of short stories by your favorite author can feel a bit too much. I know teachers who wait for summer to really dive into books that they save all year long. This type of self-sacrifice is not only unfair but it may even be hurting your practice as a teacher.

When you allow yourself the pleasure and time to read the things that nourish your reading life, you can bring those connections into your classroom. While scanning the front page of the *New York Times*, I came across a story called "The Stories That Bind Us" and even though I didn't have time to check it then, the same story popped up in my Twitter feed hours later. It felt like the story was following me throughout the day. Eventually, when I finally read it, I ended up using it for my Storytelling class, and it became a powerful experience for our learning community that would not have happened if I didn't take the time to do the reading that nourishes my teaching soul.

It is the very things that we think we don't have time for that may just sustain us through the rough patches of the year. Think about the last time you turned down an invite to coffee with a friend, seeing a concert, or going to the movies. These very things may provide you with the inspiration to find ideas and a necessary mental break from the rigors of the classroom. After all, you're providing the inspiration for so many of your students; you need to find a way to get inspired by the intellectual pleasures, art, ideas, and movements of our time.

Write for Others in Your Field

By writing about your work, your discoveries, and your insights, you also get a chance to reflect on your own practice and you get to keep a record of the work you're striving to do with your students. This reflection goes beyond mere strides toward personal improvements, it provides our society an intimate look into the complexity of teaching, and your openness allows others to have a deeper understanding of the educational challenges of our time. There are journals, blogs, and newspaper sites that love to hear from teachers in the classroom. You can give your unique perspective of how lofty policies are actually impacting the work you're doing with your students. Your point of view is important for policy makers, politicians, and parents to see and know.

Professional writing also allows you to gain a wider audience, find collaborators, and hear back from other educators on your practice. This feedback not only helps you improve your practice, but it can provide you with the encouragement to keep trying new ideas in a climate of feeling like we're under siege.

Jose Vilson sees writing about our work as a way to change public perceptions of teaching.

Jose Vilson
Math Teacher
Washington Heights, New York

Profile

Speaking up and out <u>and</u> having people actually listen is a talent, and one I constantly have to build. Writing professionally gives me the platform to say things to an audience who otherwise wouldn't seek this truth.

. . . continues

(Jose Vilson, continued)

Being a teacher writer falls in line with this too because seldom does major media reach out to teachers to talk about the context in which we work. For instance, teachers might get interviewed about a lesson plan or perhaps an event that happened at their school, but rarely do they get asked how to improve working conditions or how budget cuts affect their profession. America loves its local teachers, but only as instructor to their child, not as people who have equal parts passion and professionalism in mind for their craft.

For some reason, current teachers don't get the recognition for their expertise that other professions do. Writing about these experiences positions me (and teacher writers like me) into a slot that puts us on par with so-called education experts. At first, when I started writing, it was merely a reflective tool, a way to tell a few of my friends how I felt at work, and the sorts of things they ought to think about if they wanted to become teachers. The reflection is still there, but now my writing has made me more conscious of who I'm speaking to, people who don't necessarily get it or want to get it. How do I use my gifts to speak for teachers with similar experiences in the classroom to people who may or may not believe what we do about education?

It's amazing, really.

Use Action Research

Action research is the meeting point between classroom practice and theoretical paradigm housed in academia. When teachers take part in action research or teacher research, they rediscover their role as a learner in the process and begin to wonder how they can help their students find the same passion for inquiry, research, and reflection. It can help practitioners find their passion toward improving practice while creating new knowledge around teaching practices. Charlotte Danielson, an internationally recognized expert in the field of teacher evaluation, considers action research to be one of the tools of teachers who have reached a distinguished level of growth and professional development (1996).

On a practical level, action research is a way of problem-solving by applying research to real-world situations with the help of a learning community. McCutcheon and Jung provide the following definition for action research:

Systematic inquiry that is collective, collaborative, self-reflective, critical,
and undertaken by the participants of the inquiry. The goals of such
research are the understanding of practice and the articulation of ratio-
nale or philosophy of practice in order to improve practice. (1990, 148)

Action research can often be recursive and it may look like this; when you begin
you will start with an inquiry and plan research to tackle this inquiry (Figure 3–2).

Figure 3-2 The cycle of action research

Kemmis and McTaggart focus on the social justice aspect, describing action research as:

[a] form of collective, self-reflective inquiry undertaken by participants
in social situations in order to improve the rationality and justice of
their own social or educational practices, as well as their understand-
ings of the practices and the situations in which these practices are
carried out. Groups of participants can be teachers, students, principals,
parents, and other community members—any group with a shared
concern. The approach is only action research when it is collaborative,
though it is important to realize that the action research of the group is

achieved through the critically examined action of the individual group members. (1982, 15)

At the heart of action research are the principles of

- Working as part of a learning community.

- Applying research to real classrooms.

- Seeing teachers as the experts and honoring their findings.

- Adhering to the idea that there are many valid forms of data in teacher research (e.g., student responses, journals, focus groups, and classroom observations).

- Seeing practitioners/researchers as both being on the inside and outside of the scope of the research.

A teacher's action research not only helps to improve her practice but also broadens the knowledge base for teaching and learning.

Profile

Jennifer Isgitt
High School English Teacher
Fort Worth, Texas

Right now one of my friends and I are conducting action research on classroom discussion, specifically Harkness classroom discussion. Our biggest question is about how to adapt this method for the large class sizes that we encounter in public education. Most schools that use this method are small private schools with small class sizes, and so we have been working to figure out how to make it more effective.

Also, my friend teaches calculus, so this is a cross-disciplinary effort.

We have learned some good ways to split the class into small groups and developed some techniques and handouts for evaluating the discussion. We have developed handouts and assessment for the students who are not part of a discussion on a given day (they have a formal observation of the discussion to complete).

. . . *continues*

(Jennifer Isgitt, continued)

Action research definitely shapes my practice in the sense that I feel free to take the risk to experiment. I am very open with students about what I am doing. I tell them that I am trying something and then I ask for their feedback on how a particular practice is working. I have changed the discussion forms several times: a couple of times for the transcript form I use, and probably four or five times for the observation form I use.

Advice: Don't be afraid to try things. Let students have input into what you are doing. Explain to them that you are trying to answer a question about their learning and let them make suggestions about what would be best. Don't feel obligated to take a grade on everything. Some things won't work that well, and you shouldn't let the students suffer for that. In fact, I like to try several things before I settle on something to formally assess. Work with colleagues and share with them what you are doing. Share what you have learned with other educators!

The truth of the matter is, doing all of the things mentioned in this chapter *is more work*, at least initially, but it is the work that makes teaching an intellectual challenge, and that will give you the motivation to do your best work. Don't sell yourself short and take the intellectual fulfillment out of your job. You entered the classroom again because you love learning, so keep learning alongside your students: take on new inquiries, investigations, and new lenses. The rewards of this work will be paid with your students' success and engagement.

Presidential Medal of Freedom recipient John W. Gardner's comment about society, below, might be equally fitting for the field of education and our own classrooms:

> "[S]ociety is not like a machine that is created at some point in time and then maintained with a minimum of effort; a society is being continuously re-created, for good or ill, by its members. This will strike some as a burdensome responsibility, but it will summon others to greatness." (1995)

CHAPTER 4

Listen to Yourself

*When learning and working are dehumanized—when you
no longer see us and no longer encourage our daring, or
when you only see what we produce or how we perform—we
disengage and turn away from the very things that the world
needs from us: our talents, our ideas, and our passion.*

—Brené Brown, *Daring Greatly*

You're sitting in a late afternoon staff meeting and the topic of discussion is curbing tardiness. You remain quiet as others share their ideas aloud. Although you have some ideas that have worked—positive incentives have improved on-time attendance for your students—you hesitate and remain silent. When we retreat, due to fear or lack of confidence, we prevent innovative ideas and solutions to school-wide problems from being shared. Of course, this act of retreating from our real voice also hurts our students. As a result of our silence, we become disconnected from our work and some of us eventually burn out and leave the profession altogether.

Our identity is bound in the experiences of all those who surround us. If we want to continue to be fully engaged in our work, we need to bring our authentic voice to all spheres of our teaching. We cannot be known without having our colleagues and students see and understand our real selves. Since our identity and authenticity is tied to the perception of our work, and since our work, by nature, is constantly evaluated by ourselves, our students, and our colleagues, it is easy to see how we can become fear-based and mask our true feelings and identity. However, this disconnect may hinder our ability to act according to our values that best guide our teaching.

Although fear is a normal emotion, and one that can motivate us to be better teachers, we need to balance it with the courage to speak up when we believe our voice will benefit students. In my work with my colleagues around the country, I have found there are several common fears teachers share:

- Fear of failure in the classroom—losing control, rejection. This is probably the deepest fear: that the work we will do with our students will not matter, or even worse, they will not be invested in what we have planned. In teaching, our work is tied so closely to the relationship we build with our students that fear of rejection can render us stagnant.

- Fear of criticism from colleagues. If you have an idea to improve your school community in some way but feel like your ideas are going to go unheard, or even worse that you'll be laughed at for your idealism, then you're not likely to share your ideas with your colleagues. This is also the biggest killer of innovation.

- Fear of taking a stand. When your school leaders make decisions that do not sit well with you it is difficult to stand up and take a stand. This action can mean being ostracized or punished for naming an injustice or wrong-doing in a small community.

- Fear of having to do all the work. Perhaps the biggest fear and inhibition in creating change in schools for teachers comes from fearing that all the work will fall on your shoulders. Often, whenever you stand up to say that things can be better, you become the person who is in charge of making it a reality. You suggest more accountability for tardiness in school and suddenly you have been chosen to track tardiness and assign detentions. You think a lunch-time writing club for your students is a great idea and your principal asks you to sponsor it. Once a teacher experiences this once, he will quickly learn to stay quiet and just go back to checking his email during faculty meetings.

How Do We Manage Our Fears?

Students do not benefit from your true passion when that passion is hidden beneath layers of doubt, insecurity about being ridiculed, or fear of failure. The question becomes: How do we manage this fear to make it productive instead of corrosive? One thing that keeps my fear in check is when I channel it back into my classroom and ask students for help. For example, two nights ago, I barely slept at all. I was kept awake thinking about a new assignment that I was rolling out to my students the next day. I kept wondering if I had sufficiently prepped them for the assignment. What if the directions aren't clear? What if there is no buy-in for the assignment? What if the work produced is disappointing to me, or, and more importantly, to them? What if I fail at helping students meet the goals we've set over the past few weeks?

Instead of continuing to worry about the work we were going to do together, I turned to my students to have a discussion, as I often do, to find the places where the work needs to be tinkered, clarified, and pushed. Having honest conversations about the bumps along the road to making an idea come to life has resulted in clearer communication with students, better project results, and deeper learning. These types of conversations are possible in classrooms that view the work being done as a valuable process, where both teacher and students are co-creators in the process. I never want to become too fearful to listen to myself and follow my own instincts about classroom related decisions. I want to always be able to see the full implications of my decisions and make better ones.

How Fear Leads to Masking Our True Voice

I would like to say I always listen to my own voice and squash my fears, but this would be a lie. It can be a challenge staying open because it often leads to feelings of vulnerability. Often, this vulnerability feels like weakness and we set up ways to protect ourselves, creating a mask to protect and shield us from criticism or burn-out. However, this layer also keeps us from being completely seen or heard by our students. It also creates a barrier that blocks us from clearly seeing our students. University of Houston Professor Brené Brown has spent the past decade studying vulnerability, courage, worthiness, and shame. She defines vulnerability as "uncertainty, risk, and emotional exposure . . . [it] is the birthplace of love, belonging, joy, courage, empathy, and creativity. It is the source of hope, empathy, accountability, and authenticity" (2012, 34). When we look at the work we do with our students, it is often filled with moments of incertitude, possibility, and emotional openness. When we are faced with working in an environment where this kind of exposure is not welcomed or celebrated, we sometimes feel the pressure to protect ourselves.

When we teach in environments where authenticity and mutual trust are a rarity, there is often an unspoken code, based on our collective fears, that gets embedded in the system. The messages are implied in conversations that happen in the hallways, in between classes, in the staff lunchroom, and over lunch with colleagues. We are often told the ways we should act in these systems in confidence, as if we are being let in on a secret; we nod our heads and are even thankful for being informed. These subtle messages make an indelible impact on our minds and they shape the way we choose to be seen in our schools. They also can set up foundational beliefs which, instead of encouraging openness and vulnerability, sets us up to ignore our true voice.

Rita Sorrentino explains that she proudly wore many hats as a teacher, but she often felt that she was required to wear a mask as well.

Rita Sorrentino
Elementary Teacher, retired
Philadelphia, PA

Throughout my teaching practice, I have had to wear many hats to attend to the needs of my students; mother, counselor, detective, mediator, nurse, coach, and social worker – you get the idea. These hats have become part of my repertoire of roles, an almost second nature response, in dealing with the students and situations in and out of the classroom. Some hats have been more fitting to my personality, but all of them were worn with dignity and in good faith. I am proud of them.

On the other hand, I am not proud of the masks I have worn to get me through rough times or alleviate pressure from administrative power. I am not happy with myself when I say one thing to students but believe something else.

Each year during testing season, I am assigned to monitor a group of fifth grade students. The students arrive a bit nervous, a little apprehensive, but overall willing to give it a go. I feel like I am forced to wear a mask during the PSSA, PA State mandated testing. Sadly, I observe how the students' initial motivation and effort on day one turn into fatigue and frustration by day 3 (of 6). I encourage them (bribing them with peppermint life savers or some other award) to finish. Finish questions that they don't understand and cannot be clarified. This is a mask that adds pain to my teacher psyche. I know they know more than they are able to bubble in. I believe these tests discourage students, don't provide them with useful and timely feedback, and make the teaching and learning in our classroom less student-centered and more test prep oriented. Yet, I peek through the mask and hear myself saying to them, "Just do your best. That's all that matters." This does sound encouraging and reassuring, but I know this is not true. Just doing your best will not offset the feeling of inadequacy some students experience over the six days of testing, and it will not annihilate the trail of data and labels that will follow them for years to come.

Myths that Move Us Away from Listening to Ourselves

There are some pervasive and corrosive myths in our field that can lead to teachers setting aside what they know is best for their students (and themselves). Here are a few of the most prominent:

- **Showing emotion is a weakness.** When I first started teaching, I often heard others say that you shouldn't smile until Christmas. This might sound like good advice for a new teacher who is looking for a few clear and simple rules to live by while he or she learns the ropes. The intention behind the advice may even be good: it reminds teachers not to try to be friends with the students and, instead, to be the instructor they need teachers to be. In the short term, seeming unfazed and distant might make a teacher appear to be superhuman. In the long term, it might just appear inhuman. Most importantly, masking emotions prevents us from building a thriving classroom community.

  While we cannot completely uncover our private lives and let it interfere with our work with our students, it is unreasonable to think that our personal experiences don't color our teaching lives. We have taught on days when we have lost a family member, when our hearts have been bruised through a breakup, when we had to put a pet to sleep, or worried over our own sons and daughters who are far from home. In these moments of vulnerability, to pretend, or even assume, that we can leave the emotional experiences aside only signals to our students that we view our work with them as simply work. It is better for our students to see our authentic selves, the selves that are impacted by the emotional hurdles in our lives, than to imagine us as people without any actual troubles.

  Modeling vulnerability allows students to follow our example. What student is going to ask a question or start a conversation that might expose vulnerability in a class where the teacher models restraint? Another cost that rarely gets tallied is the effect on the teacher; it's hard to imagine not being happy seeing my students everyday, and pretending to not be excited and ecstatic about the work that we are going to do. Trying to hide or deny that enthusiasm would cost me energy and joy, both of which are essential if I want to do my job well.

- **If you are prepared, everything should go as you planned.** The idea of a controlled classroom environment where everything goes according to plan is one new teachers long for, sometimes desperately. After all, we are asked to present our most confident selves and create an appearance that we have everything together at all times. But, as any teacher who has spent some time in the classroom knows, we work with dynamic young people and we cannot control every factor impacting our classroom. While it is important that we come to work prepared, having a plan in place to organize learning activities for our students, it can be dangerous to believe that we are in control of every outcome in the classroom. It creates a huge burden, which can overpower even the best teachers. If I want my students to believe that the acronym for Fail is First Action In Learning, then I need to give myself permission to fail and improve over time as well.

Instead of thinking you can plan and control *everything*, it is better to invest your energy into thinking of each moment as a potential learning experience. It is better to learn from moments of mishap in the classroom rather than attempt the herculean task of controlling every single interaction. For example, if your students are missing major learning outcomes of big project ideas, it would behoove you to consider putting smaller deadlines and check-in points in the project process rather than to get rid of projects altogether in your classroom.

- **Perfection is the goal.** Perfection, or the pursuit of it, can be very seductive. When I first started teaching, I would compare the bulletin boards in my class to other teachers in my school. I would always bemoan the fact that mine didn't look as great as their bulletin boards. I quickly realized that bulletin boards have very little to do with actual student engagement or learning. I think the deep desire for perfection stems from comparing our work with someone else's, when we are striving for other people's approval of our work.

We create conditions in our classes that allow our students to find resiliency and a new opportunity to learn when they fail at a new skill or task. However, we do not extend this kindness to ourselves. How many nights have you spent thinking about missed opportunities to support a student, clarify a point, or plainly wished to start the day over again? Me too. Because our actions and planning impact the lives of our students, it is understandable that we feel an immense pressure and duty to do right by them. However, instead of feeling inadequate, we should be humbled by the task before us and let go of the expectation that we can perfect every lesson, every interaction with each student, and every conversation with a parent. The difference between striving for perfection and continuously honing your craft is that when you are striving for perfection, you are doing it for those on the outside. When you work toward improving your practice as a teacher, you are driven by an inherent need to do better than you did before. You are not trying to prove a point to someone else or trying to gain your self-worth from the opinion of others. When we begin to allow ourselves the same freedom to fail, we can begin to break through the walls of doubt and really begin to thrive in the classroom.

- **Administrators have the final say and they shouldn't be questioned.** After four years in the classroom, I was planning during the summer for the curriculum that I would be using in the classroom during the school year. I knew I would be tasked with teaching eleventh-grade an American Literature to my students and I realized that Mark Twain was not on the syllabus. I was aware of the difficult but relevant conversations I would need to have around language, power, and race if I were to teach Huck Finn to my students. So, I quickly began to assemble a plan. We would take an inquiry stance around the novel and our essential question would be: Is Huck Finn still relevant today? I would bring my students in contact with African American studies professors from neighboring colleges; we would Skype with the Mark Twain museum director in Missouri; we would have visits from an American Studies professor from Temple University. In short, we would take on a scholarly investigation of the relevancy of the American classic with the help of experts in the area. Our learning would culminate with a day of dialogue where my students would present their learning and hear from these esteemed scholars as well. Parents, colleagues, and other students would attend the event.

  Needless to say, I was very excited about this plan for the fall semester and was proud of myself for securing these real-world connections for my students. And then I shared the invitation for the day of dialogue with my principal. He couldn't believe my naiveté about teaching this "racist" novel at an inner city high school. He quickly called me into his office and let me know that if any parents objected to teaching this novel, I would have no support from him. He also advised me to drop my plans and avoid any controversy.

  At that time, I believed that my principal had the final say in my classroom and that there was no room for negotiation. After much soul-searching, I dropped my plans. I felt so alone, and even threatened, by the warnings admonished to me. I felt that it was better for me to keep my head down and respect my principal's wishes. If I had thought about this more at that time, I would have had a lengthier conversation with my principal and maybe would have tried to find a common ground for compromise. Looking back, I wish

I had tried harder to recruit my principal as my ally and had tried to find a way to share my plan in a way where he would have supported my efforts.

It's easy to see how an administrator can be perceived as the sole source of power—or how an administrator might even cultivate that belief. However, when we let someone's title keep us from working collaboratively with them, we not only set up power struggles like the one above, we also may edit or censor our own actions in anticipation of what the boss might think or do.

Working Toward Alignment

To be completely open and vulnerable may not be feasible for all teachers in all situations. Sometimes distance and silence are necessary because it allows us to protect ourselves from the harsh realities of working in a difficult setting so we can continue to do our job well. As the expert in your particular circumstance, you will determine your level of vulnerability based on your own judgment of the context in which you work.

No matter what your particular circumstance, I believe the essential work is to determine how we can align our teaching with our values. This means finding place, situations, and people who honor our beliefs and allow us to fail without judgment. We know what happens when we are able to let ourselves be seen by our students, to be truly present in the classroom; those moments when the class transcends boundaries of the school setting and hard-set defined roles of teachers and students and authentic learning can happen. It is only when the teacher is willing to be authentically connected to the students in the classroom that students can feel at ease and take true risks. There is no one method to be a great teacher, but you cannot be a great one till you find what Parker J. Palmer calls "your selfhood in the classroom" (1997, 7). Until your values and your actions in the classroom are aligned, you can never fully capture the imagination, intellect, and potential of your students.

How to Identify Resistance to Alignment and Overcome It

Resistance is the heavy cloak of doubt that helps us hide from the world when we need to be doing the work we are called forth to do in life. It often is hard to identify, but holds us back when we are trying to create something new in our classroom or our life. It also sneaks up on us when we are trying to change our lifestyle or habits. I believe it is the most powerful force holding us back from alignment. In his book, *The War of Art*, Steven Pressfield defines resistance as something that "cannot be touched, heard, or smelled . . . its aim is to shove us away, distract us, prevent us from doing our work." Pressfield articulates the four aspects of resistance as invisible, internal, insidious, and implacable (2002, 7).

So you're seeing the ways resistance is holding you back and how it is keeping you from achieving connectedness in the classroom. Maybe you've not applied for the teacher-leader position in your department even though you think you can contribute to your school. Maybe you've passed up an opportunity to travel to the district nearby to share how you consistently bring parent volunteers into your classroom. Perhaps you believe that you should shelve all your units from the past and start planning over this summer, but you fear the scope of this task. So, how do you overcome resistance? Pressfield offers these strategies to attack resistance and explains that resistance manifests itself in different ways throughout different points in the project:

1. To combat fear, you must *start*.

    Before you even start a novel, a new business, or commit to a new approach in your classroom, you will experience feelings of anxiety and feel that you're not ready to take on what you're about to start. Resistance will distract you, and you will find many reasons to hesitate, to remain stagnant in your typical pattern of behavior. You must push past these feelings. Goethe was right when he wrote, "Boldness has genius, power, and magic in it. Begin it now." Once you start, you will find your way.

2. To overcome uncertainty, you must *focus*.

    In the middle of any project, any work that you're doing, you will face *uncertainty*. You may even question why you started this arduous work in the first place. In these moments, you must bring clarity to your work by bringing focus to it. You will have to move closer to your work and believe that you will find your way by giving attention to it.

3. To surmount doubt, you must *finish* what you've begun.

    Near the end of any creative endeavor, you will face *doubt*. You will wonder if your work is even worth finishing. You will stall to make your work perfect, continue to tinker for improvement, and prolong sharing with others. Doubt will force you to find excuses to not finish what you've started. At any cost, you must share that presentation at the staff meeting; you must try that new approach to writing; you must send out that draft. In short, you must go public with your work and see what happens.

The bottom line is that resistance wins when you give up; when you let it reduce your drive to make something, or do something, into shreds of doubt, uncertainty, and fear. But resistance can also be your North Star. It can alert you that what you fear to do is the very thing you need to do. It lets you know that you're on the right path. Overcoming resistance can help you find alignment between what you value about teaching and learning and your actions in the classroom. For example, this past year I tried choice reading as a major part of my curriculum. When I decided to forgo the whole novel approach in my class I was faced with doubts, uncertainty, and fear. I feared that I wouldn't know how to let go of the control and help my students become lifelong readers. But letting this fear go, and starting, focusing, and finishing, I was able to help my students find their love of reading in the classroom. Even writing this book, I constantly felt resistance along the way. Many times, I felt that what I was doing was worthless and that no one would actually care about these ideas. With the help of good friends and a sage editor I was able to push through doubt to actually finish. This is my hope for you as you push past your own resistance: to have perseverance in moving toward the authentic self, both in the classroom and beyond.

Addressing External Resistance

As hard as our own internal resistance can be, sometimes the resistance manifests externally in the form of mandates from your district or state. It isn't easy to stand up to pressure from supervisors and colleagues and follow the laid out course and do things a bit differently. If you are doing something new and innovative, you are bound to ruffle some feathers, and outside pressures can move us out of alignment and away from these important ideas. But, alignment of your values and your work emboldens you to take risks and make moral and ethical decisions that go against the status quo. In these times, you will need to reach into your toolbox and choose a variety of strategies ranging from compromise to creative noncompliance to overcome the obstacles you face in the work that you want to do. It won't always be easy, but you know you're on the right path when you can hear that nagging voice of resistance, trying to stop you from the work you've set out to do with your students.

If you want to implement a strategy that is not currently being used in your school setting or by your colleagues, consider finding research or evidence from other practitioners that support the changes you want to make. Also, turn to your classroom practice and conduct practitioner research. Finally, get some support. Find out if the new strategy that you want to implement in your classroom can scale up to other classrooms, or maybe even your entire school, and ask a few colleagues to try it out with you. This creativity may open other's eyes to improve things and they may even become more receptive to other ideas you may have.

Katie McKay shares her experience with finding a slice of time where test preparation is put aside and students' authentic lives as writers is celebrated in public.

Katie McKay

Fourth-/Fifth-grade teacher

Austin Discovery School, Austin, Texas

Profile

In my eighth year teaching, I sought a bilingual fourth-grade position at my urban neighborhood school, a campus that had just been branded as "Academically Unacceptable," the lowest state accountability rating. This new label brought dozens of district officials on visits to enforce scripted curriculum.

I was handed a minute-by-minute schedule, required to teach only the subjects tested that year, and told to use test prep materials exclusively. When I asked, for example, to teach reading through the use of quality texts that could expose students to the Social Studies and Science standards, I was met with threats of "tremendous consequences."

This shortsighted and restrictive environment was hindering the growth and drive of students and teacher alike.

Twice a year, we were allowed a class party. Could our holiday celebration double as an authors' reading? The school was located within walking distance to dozens of coffee shops. I reserved a morning slot at a café and we spent recesses making invitations and posters, advertising the event. After school, I worked with students and parents in the computer lab (a space prohibited during 'instructional time') to create "identity poems," positive characteristics of the author, displayed in a colorful word cloud graphic.

Students revised their memoirs (the only genre I was permitted to teach), putting incredible thought into the effect of each word and punctuation mark, anticipating an audience who would listen, respond, and connect with their stories. They sought peer feedback and pleaded to bring their pieces home to practice reading them over and over.

. . . continues

(Katie McKay, continued)

When we arrived that day, dozens of parents, teachers, mentors, and unsuspecting patrons greeted us. We distributed colorful scraps of paper, inviting written feedback for the authors. The same kids who, at school, were associated with suspensions or failing tests, stood proudly on the stage and described themselves as clever, intelligent, cariñosa, loyal, bilingüe. The same memoirs that had begun as mere attempts to meet the expectations of a standardized rubric were revised into pieces that elicited laughter, nods of understanding, and refreshing smiles. We passed the microphone around the room, taking questions and hearing the audience's reactions.

Later, reflecting on the experience, Antoine wrote, "When I know that my writing is going to be shared with the community I read it over and over until I see the mistakes."

Eduardo said, "When I hear other students read their writing I learn that they are not mean, they are peaceful ... they learn that I am a good boy, not bad."

In those moments, students began to self-identify as intelligent and capable and to work tirelessly to make their work truly exemplary.

Katie McKay's story illustrates how we can creatively carve out a space between mandates and authentic practice that supports students. In these moments, a teacher sometimes has to choose between following the moral compass that guides her or succumbing to the mandates from above. It is a dilemma many of us have faced. How do you say no to a principal, a department chair, or even the teacher next to your classroom? For some of us, finding the middle ground will seem like selling out. For Katie, finding this compromise meant that she was able to show her students the power of their own writing, and bring a community together to rally behind her students, while following the mandates her school required. Since these choices are personal and require each of us to examine where alignment lies, the actions will vary, allowing a different course of action for each individual. Ultimately, these choices will be made based on your beliefs and you will find a way to live with them and hopefully bring yourself closer to alignment with each small action.

Be Yourself and Listen to Yourself

As a leader in the classroom, you will set yourself apart by bringing an emotional honesty to the work that you will do with your students. As you read the words from John T. Spencer, who teaches elementary school students in the Phoenix, Arizona area, think back to the story Katie shared with us and you'll notice that both of these passionate teachers bring all of themselves into the classroom. They nimbly navigate the often confusing tangles of working within a bureaucratic system. Through cultivating emotional honesty and trusting their intuition, they have found a way to align their values with their work.

I believe we all have that same kind of immense untapped potential. Once you give yourself permission to unleash that potential, you will find a way to not only improve your own practice, but help those around you as well. You will come to see that you have the unique ideas, solutions, and know-how to improve your practice, your school, even your community. When we begin to find the courage to embrace our vulnerabilities, we become a source of inspiration, not only to those who surround us, but also to ourselves.

John T. Spencer explains how he is able to bring all of his himself into the classroom.

John T. Spencer
Sixth-grade ELL teacher
near Phoenix, AZ

Profile

My faith is a deep part of what drives what I do. When I think of the core beliefs I have about teaching, they are rooted in what I believe about the Jesus story: the idea that teaching is transformative, the concept of every student as beautiful and broken, truth in paradox, the notion of redemption, the belief that there is no educational utopia, the idea that there is power in humility, the concept of grace (and the idea that teaching is, itself, a gift).

On a very practical level, my faith is why I don't believe in "good kids" and "bad kids" and why I believe humility is the solution for leading a classroom community.

Not that I always get it right. I screw up. I've yelled at kids. I've gotten impatient. But even here, it has been my faith that reminds me to be real, to apologize and to be grateful when students respond with forgiveness.

CHAPTER 5

Empower Your Students

Education is not preparation for life; education is life itself.
—John Dewey, "My Pedagogic Creed"

Our work as teachers is akin to the work of architects. While we may not build physical structures that we can visit and admire, I would argue that our legacy lasts longer in the ways our students will change the world. In your class right now, there is a future filmmaker, scientist, senator, and social worker. Your legacy, the true value of the work you do, will be measured by the way your students make a difference in your community. When they find creative solutions to problems, both local and national, you can take pride in helping nurture the next generation of change agents. And you do not have to wait years to see the benefits of empowering your students. When you put this goal at the center of the practice, you will see the payoff in your daily interaction with your students. Conversely, if you don't, that energy will drain you, instead of empowering your classroom.

For example, a number of years ago I was experiencing the mid-March low point. The weather seemed to continue to stay cold even though there were days when it seemed like spring could come at any moment. However, it was still weeks away from Easter break, and everyone at school was dragging a bit to get to the other side of it. In my classroom, everyone was a bit sluggish and we were trying, unsuccessfully, to find the energy and enthusiasm for the work ahead of us. During this time period, I was trying to teach my students important lessons about writing a research paper. They had brainstormed topics, researched resources, submitted annotated bibliographies, and even turned in rough drafts of their research papers. While the class had mustered the energy to complete the work and comprehend the mechanics of the process of writing a research paper, it still remained merely a mechanical process. Students had no ownership of their topic; they had not gone beyond the minimum requirements. At the end of the unit, I went home with about 165 research papers to grade. I was completely overwhelmed with the idea of giving substantial feedback to all my students. I left each day feeling drained and exhausted.

I knew this kind of work was not sustainable for me, nor was it best for students, so I set about trying to shift the energy of the classroom. It took me years to change my approach to teaching research and writing skills. This year, I committed to co-creating authentic experiences as readers and writers with my students. In September, we had an honest discussion about writing and seeing the role language and shaping language plays in our lives. To emphasize the point that we all use language to convey complex thoughts and feelings in playful ways, I asked my students to work in small groups to turn their text messages into poems. It led to an interesting discussion about how they are writers outside of the classroom, and whether they see themselves this way or not. Ultimately, our discussion turned to ways we can continue to hone our writing craft but do it in a meaningful way.

In this spirit, I suggested the idea of producing a teen magazine that would serve as an alternative to the traditional research project. The magazine would stand in contrast to typical teen magazines they find on grocery store shelves. We set out to produce a teen magazine that would combat stereotypes about their generation. Students enthusiastically bought into the idea and we began a quarter long process that would test our commitment along the way. Students began by finding and reading articles that could serve as mentor texts and examining them closely to learn about the ways a feature writing piece is produced for a magazine. They read about a variety of topics ranging from teen brains to perils of texting while driving. They picked up a few of the key moves writers make to grab the attention of the reader and provide useful and interesting information while maintaining an approachable tone in their writing. Once students were ready to choose their own topics for their teen magazine article, they paired up with another student or chose to work by themselves. They started researching, conducting interviews, transcribing interviews, and organizing this information for a starter draft. In addition to writing, students were divided into committees tasked with copyediting, layout, advertising, art/photography, and promotions. The biggest hurdle was coming up with a name for the magazine; students utilized a Google survey form to collect possible names and then voted on their favorite. This was the result (see Figure 5–1).

Figure 5–1 [SLA]ng Magazine

www.slideshare.net
/mkrami/mag-rami1

The biggest difference between these two teaching and learning experiences were not only how my students acquired the skills of research, writing, revising, and publishing but also how empowered they felt during the learning process. When I forced the process of writing a research paper in an artificial way, they were left powerless in what they wanted to research and how they wanted to present what they had learned through the process. When we created and published the class magazine together, we all were genuinely invested in the work we were doing as a team. Since students had a choice in what they wanted to research and write about, they were committed to writing the best piece possible. The collaborative nature of our work also helped my students see the interplay of different talents coming together in our class to create something of value, our work was not done in isolation of one and another and we came to value the diversity of strengths brought to the work. Lastly, having others see our work and react to it by providing feedback allowed the learning to continue through our reflection process. It gave us a chance to know that our work was not just for our class work but we had produced a magazine that might inspire other teens to take on a similar task. The difference in the energy that my students brought to the class during this process was palpable. It wasn't simply because we were working on a teen magazine instead of a typical research project, the collaborative process which encompassed the entire class set this experience apart from any other experience.

As for me, this experience made me realize that I have the capacity to learn new things, take chances, and experiment with how I teach writing to my students. When my students were engaged, I had more energy—both mental and physical. I was jumping out of my bed to get to school because I knew that the work we were doing together was meaningful and my students needed me to be completely present for them during the process. It made teaching pure fun for me.

A teacher is one who makes himself progressively unnecessary.

—Thomas Carruthers

The Benefits of Empowerment

Classroom practice that empowers students is deliberate, intentional, and often filled with choices that were made after thoughtful consideration of who the students are, their learning goals, and the methods which are best suited for these specific students at this specific time. When you invite students to co-create the environment in your classroom that values independent thinkers and creative problem-solvers, there are clear benefits for both you and your students.

Increased Engagement

When students create content rather than just consume it, their engagement grows capaciously. In my classroom, the students who were really turned off by reader response projects based on choice reading during the first quarter were the same ones who were the heads of committees during our teen magazine production period. They were leading tasks, supporting other students, and motivating others around them. When students have an outside audience, they have a clear purpose to get behind their own work as well as become cheerleaders for others. Although some students may struggle with the added pressure of deadlines and sharing their work widely, there are other students in class who will rise to the occasion and help their peers get there. Naturally, this increased engagement also creates a deeper connection for you with the work you're doing in the classroom. Student engagement becomes the fuel that helps keep you going even when there are challenges along the way.

Building Momentum

One of the often-unnoticed benefits of working on concrete production work with students is that it brings a palpable momentum to the classroom. No matter how engaging and committed you are as a teacher, sometimes our work feels like it drags along at some points in the year. It is yet another week where you are trying to reinforce the skills of deep reading, clear and articulate writing, and sharp thinking. When you ask your students to make, produce, and solve complex problems, you actually change the way time is experienced in the classroom. Your class shifts from staring at phones and the clock on the wall to the fast-paced workshop environment where students learn to use allotted time wisely. You must keep going despite obstacles in the way and, at times, waning enthusiasm of your students. This deadline and audience produces a momentum to your classroom so you can leverage each day of learning to its maximum capacity.

Creating a Lasting Legacy

I am finally at a point in my teaching career where my former students are writing to me three to four years out of high school and my class. They never remember the detailed lesson on in-text citation in MLA format. But, they do remember the public service announcements they produced for local nonprofits, or the readers' autobiographies we turned into a book. They never thank me for meeting the state standards for English Language Arts. But, they do thank me for remembering to ask after siblings or helping them find their love of reading and writing. You don't have to wait to hear from your students after they leave to make decisions that will make each day a meaningful one for all of you.

Even if these ideas sound right to you, the question remains: How do you go about creating the environment that will help your students cultivate the necessary habits to become change agents in their own lives and communities? Below are some goals I had for building self-empowered learning and strategies that worked for me:

Foundations That Help Teachers Empower Students

Get to know who your kids are

In order to empower our students, we first have to establish meaningful relationships with them and understand them beyond the context of test scores and numbers. Knowing your students allows you to leverage their strengths and interest when planning curriculum. It helps build a classroom community; you cannot work well with students unless you know them and their experiences in the world. Here are some strategies I use at the beginning of the year to build those relationships:

- Initiate team-building exercises to give me a chance to see how students interact. I notice the leaders, the kids who have great ideas but who won't speak up, and the ones who do not engage. I take these observations and use them in conversations at a later date.

- Administer surveys at the beginning of the year to get to know their interests and their thoughts about school.

- Listen to what kids are passionate about—in their work, in their conversations with me, in their conversations with other kids, in their choices about how they present themselves.

- Attend their sports events, performances, and school-wide activities; find out where students spend their energy in the school community.

Share responsibility and decision making with students

Getting cooperation from students can be a battle if it is set up as a power struggle, but imagine a classroom where the joys and challenges are shouldered both by teacher and students. You cannot control every interaction in the classroom, but you can certainly build a culture of respect, effort, and resilience with your students. Try these ideas to encourage this culture:

- Ask for student input when setting the norms for the classroom community.

- Choose your battles wisely; be flexible in your expectations of classroom behavior.

- Set the tone of co-ownership of all that happens in the classroom.

- Let students help you with routine tasks.

- Seek student input when developing student tasks/projects.

- Give choices in how students demonstrate what they have learned.

- Conduct a student focus group to review a unit plan or a project description before using it with the whole class.

- Create evaluation guidelines together with your students.

Model your own lifelong learning and curiosity, including the challenges

If you want your students to continue to learn long after they have left your classroom, you have to show them what it could look like. In addition, it's important for teachers to ask questions that Google cannot answer. Authentic challenges will inspire your students to take on difficult tasks. It will help them see that you value intelligence and work ethic, and provide them with work that matches their talent.

- Share what you're learning about outside of the classroom, including current reading list.

- Share your confusion about an idea, author, or experience in the world.

- Ask open-ended questions that require independent thinking, synthesis, and analysis on the part of your students.

- Model answers not based on opinion but evidence supported by reason or logic.

- Remind students that many questions do not have one correct solution.

Don't make yourself the center of the classroom

One compelling reason to empower students is it spreads the energy out to the room, so we don't have to be responsible for all of the interaction. Having to always be on can be exhausting sometimes. Make your work about the students, not about yourself. I find that when I consciously decentralize my classroom, my energy gets renewed throughout the day.

- Find ways to create conversations across students and not just with you.

- Share the responsibility for determining the best use of class time.

- Plan student seating so interaction and discussion among students is possible and encouraged.

- Seek feedback from students on best ways to handle routine tasks in the classroom.

Why Audience Matters

These strategies should help you get started in shifting the power and engagement of your classroom. If you implement these ideas, you will have changed the way your students learn; you will have created amazing content with them and you will have solved complex problems. But, none of this will have the maximum impact if you do not share their work outside of the classroom.

The students who are in front of you everyday are quite aware of their social digital capital. They track their own Twitter and Instagram followers. They have their Facebook network that intersects school, neighborhood, church, and sports teams. Cutting them off from their digital life creates feelings of disconnect which leads to disengagement. When they see schoolwork and their digital life as separate, they will not be truly invested in the work happening there. Many students adapt their digital personas based on audience. For example, their persona on mediums known to their parents such as Facebook will be more restricted while on a site like Tumblr, they are able to reveal more of themselves because that space is not populated with family members (yet). We need to take advantage of these audiences students are already populating, so we can widen their identity as writers, but also have them receive feedback that is wider than our vision.

As a teacher, I can help my students see nuances between acceptable and great writing, but my feedback is also colored by my own preferences and tastes. For example, I have a harder time connecting to readers in my classroom who are fans of the Sci-Fi genre, mainly because it isn't a genre where I am deeply invested in nor do I have the depth of knowledge that they have in it. My feedback to my students when they are reading or writing about or in this genre always feels a bit off because of my own lack of confidence to guide them through it. As teachers, our biases play a definitive role in the way we influence our students. Since we all have these blind spots and biases, we should take advantage of the opportunity to easily publish and share student work via our networks to provide broader and perhaps less-biased feedback on their work.

The reality is that your students are already producing in some digital realm. Some of them may even have a web show, or some may be trying their hand at becoming a local DJ or video producer in your community. By engaging them in a variety of writing, producing, and creating in your classroom, you are giving your students a chance to play with different types of tasks and techniques. They are able to experience the possibilities and limitations of a given genre and discover their own interests. By creating projects with a wide audience, we can facilitate developing that talent and agency.

The Art of Sharing: Finding the Right Medium

You're going to take the plunge and go public with your students' work when you feel it makes sense to do so. The level of openness of your classroom will depend on your personal comfort level, your school's culture, and your community's expectations. You do not have to make everything you do in your class public. Many educators find it helpful to start with a password-protected site before they jump into making their students' work available to anyone with Internet access.

What will you share? How will you share it?

When you're trying to decide what work, project, and student work should be shared, think of what your goal is in sharing the work in the first place.

- Are you trying to share a highlight from your classroom with parents?

- Did you try a new method to reach your students and you'd like to share your experience with your colleagues?

- Are you reflecting on your practice?

- Are you documenting the work that happens in your classroom?

There are several different platforms to consider using when you're going public with your work; here are some ways to consider using:

Blogs

You can set up a teacher blog where you periodically post your students' work and share highlights from the classroom. Your students can be guest bloggers so there are no other additional blogs to maintain. If you teach older students, and want to give each student the independence and ownership of a blog, then students can create individual blogs. It is definitely more work to manage a group of student blogs but from my experience, ownership matters, especially for older students. Sites such as Tumblr are more popular with students than a traditional blog platform such as WordPress, but often times, schools will block Tumblr because of possible inappropriate content on it. No matter what platform you choose, you need to be familiar with it, and you need to model making work public. Perhaps, begin with a blogging practice over summer and then when school begins you can slowly roll out the blogging practice in your classroom. Photographs from the classroom, captured even on your cell phone, make the stories from your classroom come to life. It is a great way to remember what actually happened in your classroom.

Video

Since so much of what happens in our classrooms is spontaneous and dynamic, the best possible way to capture it might be to capture it via video. The palpable energy of the work you do with your students will be best captured on video. These videos can be easily added to your blog or shared via email to parents and colleagues to share highlights from the classroom.

Collaboration with local publications

There are other ways to get your students' work published to a wider audience. Many local newspapers and online sites are eager to share the good news from your class and school. Are your students producing a play? Did they travel to a local historical attraction and learn something new and interesting? Have they raised funds or volunteered for a good cause lately? This would be a great story to share with your local community. By developing a relationship with a local education reporter, you can easily share the good work coming out of your classroom with your community. I recently had a chance to partner with a local site here in Philadelphia, www.phillylovenotes.com, where my students wrote love letters to Philadelphia on St. Valentine's day and the publisher of the site published a few of our letters and then linked to our school blog (Figure 5–2). We were able to get many more visitors' eyes on our work because we partnered with this local site. It was another great way to celebrate my students' effort, while giving the Philadelphia community a chance to see the work my students are producing as writers.

Figure 5–2 My students' writing online

Bringing Community Members to Your Classroom

When I taught ninth-grade students at the Franklin Learning Center in Philadelphia a number of years ago, I really wanted my students to have authentic reading and writing experiences. I also wanted my students to understand and harness the power of succinct messages. I asked my students to create public service announcements. This is a format that many of my students were familiar with, and would be challenged by creating a brief, powerful, and convincing message for social change in their community. To raise the stakes for their work and to provide a real audience for them, I asked them to research local nonprofits in the Philadelphia area and contact them to form a relationship. Essentially, my students, in small groups, became an ad agency and these local nonprofit organizations became their clients. Throughout the process of producing PSAs, representatives from these organizations either met with my students via Skype or came into school for a meeting. These meetings happened throughout the production process of the PSAs and they dealt with real issues such as crafting the message and determining the medium of the message (pamphlet vs. video PSA). Many of these organizations gave

www.phillylovenotes.com

their time and thoughtful feedback to my students so that they could perfect their public service announcements.

During these weeks, I had never seen my students more engaged; they were running into the classroom and asking if they would have time that day to work on their projects. Andre, a student who otherwise remained mostly disengaged before this unit, would come in and ask me, "Are we going to have time to work on our project today? Because, I really need to call my client at March of Dimes." Like Andre, most of my students showed interest, agency, and ownership over what they were producing. They also felt challenged by the reality of pleasing a client. Each group was made up of team members that focused on areas of creativity, logistics, graphics, copywriting, and editing. Some of the nonprofit organizations even used these PSAs on their websites.

My students' work product and ethic significantly improved over the weeks we worked on our PSAs. By connecting to real nonprofit organizations, my students were able to see a connection between their work and their community. By helping others tell their stories, they found their own voice. The value of bringing the community into the classroom ties back to John Dewey's idea that school is not just about playing life but it is life. The work that your students produce could very well change your community for the better.

This work helped me gain valuable skills of networking locally to find relevant connections for my students. I also learned how to help manage my students with these outside of the classroom connections. It isn't easy managing eight groups of students who are all at different points in the process of making a PSA but by trying this idea out, I learned how to help them manage their own workflow. Learning these skills energized me because I knew that I was becoming more effective as a teacher and a collaborator.

Ways to Expand Your Networks and Audiences

To truly empower your students to create the work that changes their communities you will need the support of local networks. The types of relationships you bring into the fold of your classroom can greatly determine the type of work your students will embrace. In some ways, this type of work can only be understood in terms of the local context of the school. For example, high school students in New York City may create a short documentary about the impact of stop-and-frisk policy on youth, while students in Ft. Worth, Texas might address how fracking is polluting their local waterways and impacting thousands of citizens in the area. As a classroom community, you will find the issues that are worthy of your attention and energy and then find local organizations in the areas willing to collaborate with your students to develop strategies for action.

Sarah Gross has used blogging to help her students become more comfortable with the idea of making their writing public. Her thoughtful approach helps us see how we can prepare our students to become writers in a connected world.

Sarah Gross

English Teacher

High Tech High School, Lincroft, New Jersey

Profile

Over the past few years, I have begun taking more of my students' work public, giving them an audience outside of just the teacher providing a grade. While grades are important to my students, I remind them that as adults they won't be receiving a report card with grades and assessments listed. Instead, the most important assessments will be informal and will be given by the audience who reads their work, whether that is their boss, a client, the grant committee, or other group responding to their work. In March I challenged my students to try the Slice of Life blogging challenge, which asked them to write twenty daily blog posts during the month. My students had been blogging on our private blogs since the beginning of the year and this time I asked them to step out of their comfort zones and create public blogs if they felt like they were ready. The results were amazing! Students went above and beyond the requirements as they watched their blog stats climb. Every morning students would enter class and shout, "I had a blog view from Germany last night!" or "Someone I don't know commented and agreed with me!" I watched as their blog posts improved by leaps and bounds over the course of the month, with their voices becoming more distinct and their writing stronger. At the end of the month, I surveyed them about their experiences. When asked about the process of blogging, one student said, "I loved it! I got feedback from people I didn't know, and learned from what they had to say. It was great to get the interaction, and it really made my experience enjoyable." What more could a teacher ask for? That same student said that he began to edit and revise more as he saw his audience growing. As a teacher, I struggle to get my students to revise and edit, because they just don't see it as important. But that changes when they have an active audience outside the classroom!

. . . continues

(Sarah Gross, continued)

My favorite reflection came from a student who characterized himself as a non-writer at the beginning of the year. He blogged on our Ning during the challenge and at the end he told me, "I learned that I actually CAN write. Who would've thought?" And isn't that what we all want our students to realize? Sometimes, it doesn't matter how many times we praise them and encourage them because they tune out the teacher voice. But when their classmates and other readers online comment on their writing? That means something, and they take it to heart. So be brave and help your students be brave, too—take your writing public and help them do the same!

There are probably several different types of partnerships you can form to help your students connect what they are learning to the world around them. You may want to be strategic and think about what your needs are and then look for meaningful connections for your classroom.

Arts organizations

Are your students performing a play? Are they learning how to paint a mural? Do you have a local arts organization that would support an artist-in-residence program at your school? Or better yet, would an organization love to give your little artists a chance to collaborate with a professional artist and create public art for your community? Investigate your local arts organizations and see how they are looking to connect your classroom to the work that they are doing in the community.

Political and community leaders

Elected leaders and local civic organizations are great places to turn to when your students are learning about history, economics, and citizenship. Imagine having your local business council evaluate your students' startup plans. Or what would it look like if your speech class had a guest appearance from an elected official who talks to your class about crafting and delivering a message effectively? Often, these leaders are more than happy to share their experience.

Joshua Block

History Teacher

Science Leadership Academy, Philadelphia, Pennsylvania

Profile

Partnerships with art and community organizations have allowed me to dramatically increase and improve the learning experiences that I design for my students. An annual collaboration with a dance company has exposed my students to the concept and the process of creating site-specific dance. The students have then used these newly acquired skills to create (in consultation with professional dancers) performance pieces that are part of a citywide arts festival.

During a playwriting unit my students receive feedback from a professional playwright as they write new scenes. The first time that they receive detailed feedback they respond with astonishment and pride. "She really read it!" "Her comments really made me think about what I want to happen next [in my play]."

The partnerships that I have established with professionals and organizations have exposed my students to new possibilities and challenged my students to bring their best selves to their work. When students understand that a project is for a larger audience and that there are others, besides their regular teacher, who is invested in the work and eager to assist them, then student motivation increases and the quality of the work produced increases. I have seen students who are not always highly engaged bask in compliments and appreciations offered by professionals in response to work they have created.

One key element for me of successful partnerships has been to plan collaboratively. At times the planning has been difficult because our visions have not necessarily overlapped. At these moments I have to remind myself to be flexible but also remember that I know my students and the goals of my classroom the best. I try to find ways to express myself clearly and attempt to work with the collaborator to find common ground—ways that their skills can be used to successfully enrich the learning and work of students. Ultimately, once we have a shared vision and open channels of communication we can move forward and challenge students to embark on new experiences in meaningful ways.

Career experts

For any career path your students want to pursue in the future, you can help them to connect with a local expert/mentor in the field. Your students can explore careers in technology, medicine, law, and business by finding internships within your local community. By connecting your students to local experts in the area, you're bringing their interests to life. You're also providing them with possible life-long mentorships and guidance for the dreams they want to pursue. To your community, you're making your students' work visible and helping people realize that all kinds of amazing work is happening there.

Is It Worth It?

No work worth doing is without its challenges, and you will certainly encounter them when you think about ways to empower your students. There might not be a culture of sharing and openness at your school, and you might make your colleagues feel uncomfortable by simply promoting your students' work. There may even be feelings of jealousy or animosity if your colleagues feel threatened by the attention you receive for your work. In these moments of doubt and discomfort, you will have to decide if the risk of going public is worth the rewards it brings to your students and your own practice. There are several different reasons why you may find this to be difficult work.

Aren't Empowered Students More Difficult to Control?

The short answer is: yes. But again, if your end goal is to help your students become life-long, independent thinkers, learners, and doers then you will find ways to overcome the challenges you will face together on this path. Instead, building productive relationships and challenging your students to create meaningful work together will result in true fulfillment in your work. I have had as many as thirty-three students in a classroom; trying to control them will only lead to needless battle. But, investing energy in doing meaningful work together can make a huge difference.

Is It More Work?

The cycle of teaching doesn't end with handing papers back and closing your grade book at the end of the day when you go public with your work. You may have to reach out to local contacts to promote your students' work. You may have to respond to emails. You may even have to look for such connection for the sharing to be possible. However, your students will receive richer feedback and you may gain a variety of perspectives on your students' work rather than relying on your own sole judgment to view the work your students are doing. This infusion of voices will give you energy in spite of the extra steps you may have to take to get there. In the end, the pride that your students will have for knowing that their work lives beyond the four walls of your classroom might just make all the extra work worthwhile.

What About Errors?

Naturally, when you go public with your work, there's trepidation that others will judge it unfairly. Will your students spell everything correctly? Will the work be less than perfect? Will you be judged by their production? These are all valid and fair questions to ask. When you go public with your students' work, try to remember that their work is just one iteration of many in your class, or as Paul Valery wrote, "no poem is ever finished, it is only abandoned" (1966, 74). The same is true of the writing that happens in your classroom. Your goal for sharing is to share the learning process along the way; this is not an exhibition of best essays on *Romeo and Juliet* ever written. Not everything you do in the classroom will make sense to share with the wider public. But, if you never share, the work will just live and wither away in your classroom. By taking the risk of sharing, you're also modeling the openness and vulnerability needed in all true learning.

How Do I Find Resources?

You do not have to do this work alone. From the very first back-to-school night, encourage colleagues and parents to help you build meaningful connections for your students in the community. Attend local events and always be on the lookout for someone who would bring interesting learning experiences to your students. In this day and age of constant budget cuts and insurance red tape, do not become daunted by school trips. Take as many as you can and help your students truly see that you're not playing school along with them, but that you're helping them become prepared to take on the most pressing issues of their community, city, and country.

My colleagues Melanie Manuel and Joshua Block turned snippets from their students' language biographies into public art, making the faces and voices of our students a presence on a Philadelphia street.

Figure 5–3   Science Leadership Academy's Inside Out Project

Josh describes the project: "As a Spanish and an English teacher working together, we developed inquiry units related to themes of language, identity, and public art. Our goals were to have students transform a public space and present their multiple identities, stories, and insights to the city around us. We were motivated to do this project, in part, by the fact that so many of the public images of youth are narrow in scope and negative in tone."

According to Jalisa, one of the students featured in the project, "We had the chance to express ourselves in the mural. We are expressing who we are and where we come from, our backgrounds, and how our language influences them."

Empowering students is the final frontier in teaching: it lets you bring your energy, commitment, and brilliant ideas, but keeps your students at the center of your practice. When your students are empowered, they have opportunities to gather knowledge, wisdom, and even empathy. They are engaged, invested, and fearless in the risk-taking that all meaningful learning experiences require. In short, they are exactly what the world—and life—demands of them. If our success is measured by their success, empowering builds our legacy as educators.

We Shall Thrive

Although some teachers might think I am crazy for saying this, I believe this is the best moment to be a teacher. Despite attacks on our profession, union-busting that is rampant around the country, and unrelenting focus on standardization rather than individualization in schools, there is a lot of amazing and exciting work being done in our classrooms around the country. Like an elderly auntie who tries to fit a lifetime of advice into her goodbyes, there are so many things I'd like you to remember after you close this book:

- There are people in your community and network who want to help you and who want to be a part of your classroom and your students' lives. They can help you if you invite them.

- Know your students well so that you can live in peace with the decisions you make for them.

- Although the tools will come and go, how you model lifelong learning will stay with your students long after they leave your classroom.

- Standing still in these times is not an option. Your teaching must change and respond to the evolving world around you.

- You may not see immediate results or gratification with your students, but eventually you will. Watch for the tiny moments and appreciate them.

- You don't have to follow every mandate put in front of you.

- Teaching is incredibly difficult and it is the most meaningful work you'll ever do in your life. It will challenge you physically, emotionally, and intellectually, and nothing you've ever done before will completely prepare you for it.

But if you remember only one thing from this book, please remember this: No matter where you began your teaching journey, where it goes next is up to you. You have the power to construct the next phase or passage of your teaching career. You have the power to decide how you will find joy and energy in your work and how you will help your students shape the future. I'm humbled to be on the journey with you.

Bibliography

Baker-Doyle, Kira J. 2011. *The Networked Teacher: How New Teachers Build Social Networks for Professional Support.* New York, NY: Teachers College Press.

Brandt, Ronald S. 1986. "On the Expert Teacher: A Conversation with David Berliner." *Educational Leadership,* 44 (2): 4–9.

Broad Foundation, The. "The Education Crisis: Statistics." Available at www .broadeducation.org/about/crisis_stats.html. Accessed September 12, 2013.

Brown, C. Brene. 2012. *Daring Greatly: How the Courage to Be Vulnerable Transforms the Way We Live, Love, Parent, and Lead.* New York, NY: Gotham Books.

Burke, Jim. 2010. *What's the Big Idea? Question-Driven Units to Motivate Reading, Writing, and Thinking.* Portsmouth, NH: Heinemann.

———. 2012. *The English Teacher's Companion: A Completely New Guide to Classroom, Curriculum, and the Profession.* 4th Ed. Portsmouth, NH: Heinemann.

Center for Comprehensive School Reform and Improvement. 2009. "Professional Learning Communities." Available at www.ldonline.org/article/Professional _Learning_Communities?theme=print. Accessed September 5, 2013.

Corncordia University of Saint Paul, College of Education. "Teacher Education Conceptual Framework." www2.csp.edu/coe/About_Us/Conceptual _Framework.html. Accessed October 28, 2013.

Csikszentmihalyi, Mihaly. 2000. *Beyond Boredom and Anxiety: The Experience of Play in Work and Games.* San Francisco: Jossey-Bass Publishers.

———. 2008. *Flow: The Psychology of Optimal Experience.* New York, NY: Harper & Row.

Daniels, Harvey, and Steven Zemelman. 2004. *Subjects Matter: Every Teacher's Guide to Content-Area Reading.* Portsmouth, NH: Heinemann.

Danielson, Charlotte. 1996. *Enhancing Professional Practice: A Framework for Teaching.* Alexandria, VA: Association for Supervision and Curriculum Development.

Darling-Hammond, Linda. "Recruiting and Retaining Teachers: What Matters Most and What Can Government Do?" Available at www.forumforeducation .org/news/recruiting-and-retaining-teachers-what-matters-most-and-what -can-government-do. Accessed September 5, 2013

Dewey, John. 1897. "My Pedagogic Creed." *School Journal* 54: 77–80.

Dewitz, Peter, and Jonni Wolskee. 2012. *Making the Most of Your Core Reading Program: Research-Based Essentials.* Portsmouth, NH: Heinemann.

Gardner, John W. 1995. *Self-Renewal: The Individual and the Innovative Society.* New York, NY: Norton.

Good, Thomas L., and Jere E. Brophy. 2008. *Looking in Classrooms.* Boston: Pearson/Allyn and Bacon.

Ingersoll, Richard M. 2012. "Beginning Teacher Induction: What the Data Tell Us." *Phi Delta Kappan* 93 (8): 47–51.

Kanter, Rosabeth M. 2001. *Evolve! Succeeding in the Digital Culture of Tomorrow.* Watertown, MA: Harvard Business Review Press.

———. 2013. "The Happiest People Pursue the Most Difficult Problems." Available at http://blogs.hbr.org/2013/04/to-find-happiness-at-work-tap/. Accessed November 18, 2013.

Kemmis, Stephen, and Robin McTaggart. 1982. *The Action Research Planner.* Waurn Ponds, Vic.: Deakin University, Open Campus Program, School of Education.

Kopkowski, Cynthia. 2008. "Why They Leave." Available at www.nea.org /home/12630.htm. Accessed September 5, 2013.

McCutcheon, Gail, and Burga Jung. 1990. "Alternative Perspectives on Action Research." *Theory into Practice* 29 (3): 144–51.

Palmer, Parker J. 1997. "The Heart of a Teacher." *Change Magazine*, November/ December 1997, 14–21.

Pink, Daniel H. 2009. *Drive: The Surprising Truth About What Motivates Us.* New York, NY: Riverhead Books.

Pressfield, Steven. 2002. *The War of Art: Break Through the Blocks and Win Your Inner Creative Battles.* New York, NY: Black Irish Entertainment.

Reagans, Ray, and Ezra W. Zuckerman. 2001. "Networks, Diversity and Performance: The Social Capital of R&D Teams." *Organization Science* 12 (4): 502–17.

Surowiecki, James. 2004. *The Wisdom of Crowds: Why the Many Are Smarter than the Few and How Collective Wisdom Shapes Business, Economies, Societies, and Nations.* New York, NY: Doubleday.

Turnbull, H.W. 2008. *The Correspondence of Isaac Newton, Volume 1.* Cambridge, U.K.: Cambridge University Press.

U.S. Department of Education. Office of Educational Technology. 2010. *Transforming American Education: Learning Powered by Technology.* Available at www.ed.gov/sites/default/files/NETP-2010-final-report.pdf. Accessed October 28, 2013.

———. 2011. "Connect and Inspire: Online Communities of Practice in Education." Available at http://connectededucators.org/report/files/2011/03/0143_OCOP-Main-report.pdf. Accessed October 28, 2013.

Valery, Paul. 1966. *The Princton University Chronicle* 26 (1): 10.

Wessling, Sarah Brown. 2013. "Confessions of a *Real* Teacher." Available at http://blogs.edweek.org/edweek/rick_hess_straight_up/2013/03/confessions_of_a_real_teacher.html. Accessed November 18, 2013.